The Lakehouse Effect

A New Era for Data Insights and AI

Steven Astorino

Mark Simmonds

MC Press Online, LLC

Boise, ID 83703 USA

The Lakehouse Effect: A New Era for Data Insights and AI

Steven Astorino and Mark Simmonds

First Edition
First Printing – March 2024

MC Press offers excellent discounts on this book when ordered in quantity for bulk purchases or special sales, which may include custom covers and content particular to your business, training goals, marketing focus, and branding interest.

MC Press Online, LLC
Corporate Offices: 3695 W. Quail Heights Court, Boise, ID 83703-3861 USA
Sales and Customer Service: (208) 629-7275 ext. 500
service@mcpressonline.com
Permissions and Bulk/Special Orders: mcbooks@mcpressonline.com
www.mcpressonline.com • www.mc-store.com

ISBN: 978-1-58347-907-0
Printed in Canada

CONTENTS

ACKNOWLEDGMENTS

A special thank you to our contributors and collaborators, who helped make this book possible:

IBM contributors:

- *Vikram Murali, for his many lakehouse insights*

- *Luv Aggarwal, for his analogy of restaurants to data lakes and data warehouses*

- *Manish Bhide, for his description of data governance and AI governance in lakehouses*

- *Roger E. Sanders, for preparation of illustrations, peer review of this book, and editing skills*

External contributors:

- *MC Press Online, for their editorial reviews and publishing*

PREFACE

Many new paradigms and advances in computing technologies have sought to revolutionize the ways in which organizations analyze and extract insights from data. Over time, consumers learn the values and limitations of these technologies. Some technologies have a short life span. Others endure and evolve over decades and remain relevant to this day, such as relational database management systems (RDBMSs).

Accurate and accessible data, in all its forms—structured, unstructured, multimedia, digital, genetic, organic—is the lifeblood of Artificial Intelligence (AI). With the right data, AI can help accelerate achievement of smarter outcomes and discover innovative ways of solving some of the world's most challenging business and societal problems, if implemented correctly and ethically.

Yet many, if not all, organizations continue to face challenges of managing, governing, and analyzing sprawling disparate data silos spread across their multi-vendor on-premises, private, public cloud, and hybrid multi-cloud environments. Much of this is discussed in our previous publications, *Artificial Intelligence: Evolution and Revolution* and *Data Fabric: An Intelligent Data Architecture for AI*, both available at MC Press Bookstore (mc-store.com).

This book attempts to explain the concepts and values that a *lakehouse* can deliver. A lakehouse couples the cost benefits and versatility of data lakes with the data structure and high-performance data management capabilities of data warehouses into a single unified data store that can be consistently and efficiently accessed, governed, analyzed, and consumed by AI applications. This book is intended for technical communities, such as developers, data scientists, and C-level IT executives, as well as business communities, such as business managers requiring self-service analytics/AI, and C-level business executives.

As we explain the lakehouse concept from the viewpoint of our combined industry experience of more than 60 years, we hope you gain value and knowledge from our thoughts and insights.

While this book refers to some IBM products and approaches, it is not intended to endorse any product or company, although it draws from our own experiences of products that we have been exposed to during our journeys. The opinions expressed herein are our own and not those of any company for which either of us has worked.

Finally, we would like to thank our friends, our contributors, and, most of all, our families for their patience while we wrote this book. We hope you enjoy reading it as much as we enjoyed writing it.

Our best,

Steven Astorino and Mark Simmonds

> *"No matter how busy you may think you are, you must find time for reading, or surrender yourself to self-chosen ignorance."*
> — *Confucius: 551 BC–479 BC*

1

EVOLUTION OF DATA

Data surrounds us. Every cell of every lifeform holds data of some sort. From the moment we are born, our senses send signals (data) to our brain that we continually process, creating yet more data as part of our thought processes. It's a never-ending cycle. To provide a context, it may be helpful to briefly explore how modern data processing evolved.

Since the beginning of earliest civilizations, humankind has sought to share its thoughts and experiences with others through symbols, such as drawings on cave walls, hieroglyphs in tombs, ancient scrolls, papers, and books. As a species, our passion to learn and progress has led to the desire and need to capture all this data, to store and share it for posterity, and to pass our collective knowledge on to others as a means of building a civilization. The establishment of education delivered through scholastic programs and institutions helped formalize what we learn and how we learn. Educational, governmental, medical, public, and other organizations established their own libraries (the earliest forms dating back to 2600 BC), holding vast quantities of information, accessible for reference or for lending to patrons. Catalogs of this information have helped provide an indexed virtual representation of what is available, how it is stored, and where to find it. Library patrons have also benefitted from the expert assistance offered by librarians or library technicians.

Early Data Storage and Management

Decades ago, analog recordings of audio, photographs, and videos presented new dimensions of capturing data. Punched cards for gathering and processing early census data using tabulating machines appeared. Recorded music on 78 rpm platters and "wire recorders" became a mainstay of radio. Magnetic tape emerged from the laboratory.

Information storage in most people's minds at the end of the World War II era meant books, filing cabinets, or, to those at the leading edge of data-processing technology, paper punch cards. At that time, reels of tape, tape cartridges, and programmable computers were the stuff of science fiction. In 1952, IBM announced the IBM 726, its first magnetic-tape unit, as shown in Figure 1.1. It shipped with the IBM 701 Defense Calculator. This innovation was significant because it was the first IBM large-scale electronic computer manufactured in quantity and was:

- IBM's first commercially available scientific computer

- The first IBM machine in which programs were stored in an internal, addressable, electronic memory

- Developed and produced in record time (less than two years from "first pencil on paper" to installation)

- Key to IBM's transition from punched-card machines to electronic computers with tape storage

Figure 1.1: An IBM 700 Series

The IBM 701 Electronic Data Processing System included the IBM 701 electronic analytical control unit, IBM 706 electrostatic storage unit, IBM 711 punched-card reader, IBM 716 printer, IBM 721 punched-card recorder, IBM 726 magnetic-tape reader/recorder, IBM 727 magnetic-tape unit, IBM 731 magnetic-drum reader/recorder, IBM 736 power frame #1, IBM 737 magnetic-core storage unit, IBM 740 cathode-ray-tube output recorder, IBM 741 power frame #2, IBM 746 power distribution unit, and IBM 753 magnetic-tape control unit.

What followed was the advent of digital disk storage, which enabled organizations to collect and process more data faster than ever. In 1968, IBM launched the world's first commercial database-management system, called Information Control System and Data Language/Interface (ICS/DL/I). In 1969, it was renamed as Information Management System (IMS).

IBM's Database 2 traces its roots back to the beginning of the 1970s when Edgar F. Codd, a researcher working for IBM, described the theory of relational databases and, in June 1970, published the model for data manipulation.

In 1974, the IBM San Jose Research Center developed a relational Database Management System (DBMS), called System R, to implement Codd's concepts. A key development of the System R project was Structured Query Language (SQL), although it was initially named Structured English Query Language (SEQUEL). The SQL data-management language for relational databases is still in use today.

The name "DB2" was first given to the DBMS in 1983 when IBM released DB2 on its MVS mainframe platform. More information on the history of Db2 is available at https://www.ibm.com/blog/the-hidden-history-of-db2/.

IBM and many other vendors continue to invest in relational and other forms of databases as they are one of the key technologies in online transactional processing (OLTP). IBM Db2, as it is known today, is also used for transaction analytics processing.

Relational databases have become the core technology for data warehouses and Master Data Management (MDM) systems (MDM systems are described below). In parallel to relational databases, other forms of data stores appeared, such as object-oriented, NoSQL, key value, wide-column store, and graph databases, to name but a few.

From Centralized to Distributed

For many years, data storage and processing were centralized. People had to take their work to the computer or access it through "dumb" terminals. With the advent of more-affordable computers, processing and data became decentralized, putting computing power in the hands of individuals. However, this led to a problem of data being replicated in an uncontrolled manner.

With data being created, stored, and processed across many personal devices, it became increasingly difficult to control the sprawl of versions of data sets and apply quality, security, and other controls. It didn't take long for individual departments in various enterprises to start organizing and storing just the data they needed, which gradually resulted in the problem of creating many data silos that usually didn't communicate with each other across an organization.

Master Data Management (MDM) is the discipline by which business and information technology work together to ensure the uniformity, accuracy, stewardship, semantic consistency, and accountability of the enterprise's official shared master-data assets. Combined with data warehousing, MDM helps provide a 360-degree view of a data entity, such as a person or product. (The reference to 360-degree view implies users should be able to look at an entity from many different perspectives to form a more complete understanding of it.) In a sense, MDM's creation was an attempt to recentralize some of the key data that was being held in disparate silos so it could be used across the whole organization as a trusted source of data—a single version of the truth, if you will. However, it still left the problem that there were often prime copies and distributed secondary copies of the data that needed to be kept synchronized to provide a truly trustworthy data source.

Data Stores, Data Integration, and Data Management Tools

Subsequently, numerous solutions appeared for managing and integrating data in order to enable reporting, analysis, and discovery of insights as data volumes grew. All of them were data stores given names such as database, online transactional processing (OLTP), online analytical processing (OLAP), data warehouse, MDM system, data mart, data lake, data lakehouse, and Hadoop. These terms tend to be used somewhat interchangeably at times, but while the terms are similar, important differences exist that are explained below. Each provides certain capabilities and values to different groups of users, but none is a panacea for all data management challenges, as originators hoped for when each was created. However, technology follows a maturity curve or cycle, and these technologies eventually found their own niches as they matured.

Many forms of data stores and data servers are being used across the enterprise today. More variations of these, and new paradigms, will evolve in the future because technology is constantly advancing. The authors of this book believe a data fabric (an architectural approach that simplifies data access in an organization and facilitates self-service data consumption, as discussed in our *Data Fabric* book at MC Press Bookstore (mc-store.com)) can offer enough longevity and flexibility to be able to integrate an organization's current and future data assets and enable them for AI applications.

Data Warehouse

The data warehouse, or enterprise data warehouse (EDW), is a system that aggregates data from different sources, integrating it into a single, central, consistent data store to support data analysis, data mining, AI, and machine learning (ML). A data warehouse system enables an organization to run analytics on huge volumes (terabytes and petabytes) of historical data in ways that a standard database cannot. Aggregating data from different sources into a single warehouse also enables transactional systems to retain sub-millisecond performance while data analysis is concurrently being performed on the warehouse.

Data warehousing systems have been a part of business intelligence (BI) solutions for more than three decades, but their evolution has continued with the recent emergence of new data types and data-hosting methods. Traditionally, a data warehouse was hosted on premises—often on a mainframe computer—and its functionality was focused on extracting data from other sources, cleansing and preparing that data, and loading and maintaining the data within a relational database. More recently, a data warehouse might be hosted on a dedicated appliance or in the cloud, and most data warehouses have added analytics capabilities and data visualization and presentation tools.

A data warehouse provides a foundation for the following:

- **Better data quality:** A data warehouse centralizes data from a variety of data sources, such as transactional systems, operational databases, and flat files. It then cleanses the data set (by fixing incorrect, incomplete, or otherwise erroneous data and eliminating duplicate records) and standardizes it to create a single source of the truth.

- **Faster business insights:** Data from disparate sources limits the ability of decision-makers to set business strategies with confidence. Data warehouses enable data integration across such differing sources, enabling business users to leverage all of a company's data into each business decision.

- **Smarter decision-making:** A data warehouse supports large-scale BI functions such as data mining (finding unseen patterns and relationships in data), AI, and ML—tools data professionals and business leaders can use to get hard evidence for making smarter decisions in virtually every area of the organization.

- **Gaining and growing competitive advantage:** All the above combine to help an organization by finding more data opportunities more quickly than is possible from older methods using disparate data stores.

Data Warehouses and Online Analytical Processing (OLAP)

In a data warehouse environment like the one shown in Figure 1.2, relational databases can be optimized for OLAP to facilitate analysis, enable queries on large numbers of records, and summarize data in many ways. Data stored in the data warehouse can also come from multiple sources.

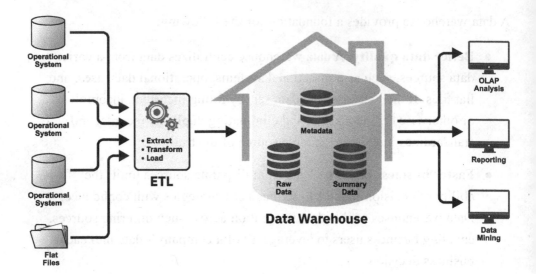

Figure 1.2: A typical data warehouse architecture

Online Analytical Processing (OLAP) vs. Online Transactional Processing (OLTP)

The main distinction between OLAP and OLTP is reflected in their names: analytical vs. transactional. Each system is optimized for that type of processing. OLAP is optimized to conduct complex data analysis for smarter decision-making. OLAP systems are designed for use by data scientists, business analysts, and knowledge workers, and they support BI, data mining, and other decision-support applications. OLTP, on the other hand, is optimized to process a massive number of transactions. OLTP systems are designed for use by frontline workers (e.g., cashiers, bank tellers, hotel desk clerks) or for customer self-service applications (e.g., online banking, e-commerce, travel reservations).

Other key differences between OLAP and OLTP include:

- **Focus:** OLAP systems enable users to extract data for complex analysis. To drive business decisions, the queries often involve large numbers of records. In contrast, OLTP systems are ideal for making simple updates, insertions, and deletions in databases. The queries typically involve just one or a few records.

- **Data source:** An OLAP database has a multidimensional schema, so it can support complex queries of multiple data facts from current and historical data. Different OLTP databases can be the source of aggregated data for OLAP, and they may be organized as a data warehouse. OLTP, on the other hand, uses a traditional DBMS to accommodate a large volume of real-time transactions.

- **Processing time:** In OLAP, response times are orders of magnitude slower than in OLTP. Workloads are read-intensive, involving enormous data sets. For OLTP transactions and responses, every millisecond counts, so OLTP workloads involve simple read and write operations via Structured Query Language (SQL), requiring less time and less storage space.

- **Availability:** Because they don't modify current data, OLAP systems can be backed up less frequently. However, OLTP systems modify data frequently. It is the nature of transactional processing to require frequent or concurrent backups to help maintain data integrity.

Data Warehouse vs. Transactional Database

As mentioned, a database is built primarily for fast queries and transaction processing rather than analytics. A database typically serves as the focused data store for a specific application, whereas a data warehouse stores data from any number (or even all) of the applications in an organization. A database focuses on updating real-time data while a data warehouse typically has a broader scope, capturing current and historical data for predictive analytics, ML, and other advanced types of analyses.

Data warehouses are good foundations for a data system that uses AI and a data-fabric architecture for several reasons:

- Transactional databases are typically smaller and grow to only a few terabytes of data. The larger they grow, the larger the performance impact. Data warehouses are typically several hundred terabytes and can grow to petabytes.

- There is a need to access and analyze data from many different sources to provide data scientists or business analysts with the ability to make better decisions by leveraging different types of data.

- Running analytical queries has a performance impact on any computer system and can take anywhere from multiple seconds to many minutes (and in some cases longer) to execute. While this is acceptable for reporting and BI, it is not acceptable for real-time transactions. Taking a banking transaction as an example, a user could be frustrated by having to wait several minutes to withdraw cash or deposit a check. Because of the impact on performance by analytical queries on a transactional database, moving data to a warehouse becomes the norm and hence the need for these two systems.

Disadvantages of a Data Warehouse

The disadvantages of a data warehouse are centered around the multiple complexities that can result when data needs to be moved or replicated regularly, as data warehouses often require. These include costs, the fact that data is typically out of date or out of synch, and slower performance. Security issues can include the need to provide data protection to multiple environments and the problem that, as additional users gain access to the data warehouse, that access creates security risks to personally identifiable, confidential, and sensitive data.

Data Warehouse vs. Data Lake

A data warehouse gathers raw data from multiple sources into a central repository, structured using predefined schemas (for example, predefined tables, each having a set of defined columns or fields) designed for data analytics. A data lake can be considered a data warehouse without the predefined schemas and often is much larger than warehouses, reaching multi-petabyte scale and higher. As a result, a data lake enables more types of analytics than a data warehouse, as it supports the storage of data in many different formats as and when new data needs to be stored. Data lakes are commonly but not exclusively built on big-data platforms such as Apache Hadoop (defined below).

Data Warehouse vs. Data Mart

A data mart is a subset of a data warehouse that contains data specific to a particular business line or department. Because they contain a smaller subset of data, data marts enable a department or business line to discover insights focused on their users' specific needs more quickly than possible when working with the broader data warehouse data set.

Data Warehouse Appliance

A data warehouse appliance is a pre-integrated bundle of hardware and software (CPUs, storage, operating system, and data warehouse software) that a business can connect to its network and start using as is. A data warehouse appliance sits somewhere between the cloud and on-premises implementations in terms of upfront cost, speed of deployment, ease of scalability, and management control.

Apache Hadoop

Apache Hadoop is a collection of open-source software utilities that facilitates using a network of many computers to solve problems involving massive amounts of data and computation. The ecosystem is shown in Figure 1.3. It provides a software framework for distributed storage and processing of large data sets using the MapReduce programming model.

Hadoop was originally designed for use with computer clusters built from commodity hardware, which is still the most common use. It has since also found use on clusters of higher-end hardware. All the modules in Hadoop are designed with a fundamental assumption that hardware failures are common occurrences and should be automatically handled by the framework.

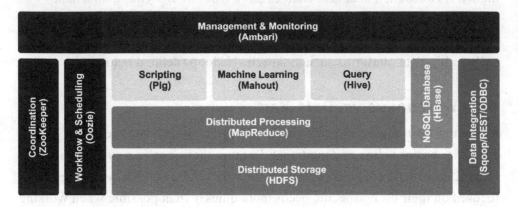

Figure 1.3: Apache Hadoop ecosystem

The core of Apache Hadoop consists of a storage part, known as Hadoop Distributed File System (HDFS), and a processing part, which is a MapReduce programming model. Hadoop splits files into large blocks and distributes them across nodes in a cluster. It then transfers packaged code into nodes to process the data in parallel. This facilitates concurrent processing by splitting petabytes of data into smaller chunks and processing them in parallel on Hadoop commodity servers. Once processing is complete, Hadoop aggregates all the data from multiple servers to return a consolidated output back to the application.

This approach takes advantage of data locality, under which nodes manipulate the data they can access. This enables the data set to be processed faster and more efficiently than it would be within a more conventional supercomputer architecture that relies instead on a parallel file system in which computation and data are distributed via high-speed networking. Hadoop is considered by many to be a form of data lake.

Data Lake vs. Lakehouse

A data lake, as shown in Figure 1.4, is a centralized data repository for management of extremely large data volumes and serves as a foundation for collecting and analyzing data in its native format(s), whether that data is structured (such as relational database records), semi-structured (records with some structure, while enabling storage of different data types and sources), or unstructured (which may include multimedia and conversational free text). This can help organizations derive new insights, make better predictions, and achieve improved optimization. Unlike traditional data warehouses, data lakes can process video, audio, logs, texts, social media, and sensor data, as well as data and documents to power apps, analytics, and AI.

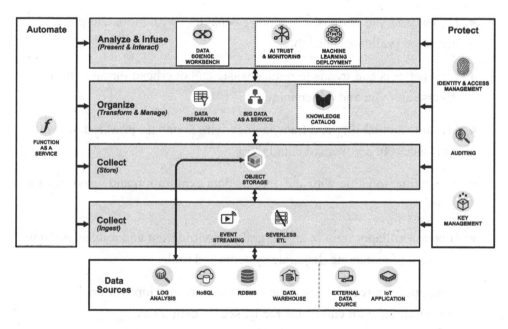

Figure 1.4: Example data lake architecture

Data warehouses and data lakes each evolved to meet a set of specific technology and business needs and values. As organizations often need both, there has been increasing demand for a convergence of both technologies. Thus, the lakehouse was born. A lakehouse couples the cost benefits of a data lake with the data structure and data management capabilities of a data warehouse. It is an evolution of the analytic data repository that supports acquisition to refinement, delivery, and storage with an open table format. Without going into detail, it is defined as part of Apache Iceberg (see https:// iceberg.apache.org) and was designed for handling huge analytic data sets. It is used in production where a single table can contain tens of petabytes of data and the data can be read without a distributed SQL engine.

Lakehouses are designed to help organizations get more from their existing investment in data warehouses and data lakes. It supports the existence of both through access to and management of a larger variety of combined data for increased flexibility. Lakehouses can provide users with the following abilities:

- Understand and anticipate customer behaviors with more complete, governed (validated) insights.

- Spot patterns and trends to reduce waste and overhead through more diverse analytic and AI techniques.

- Promote auditability and transparency with metadata-powered, native data access in a governed data lake.

- Speed time to value with self-service data exploration and discovery for users.

- Increase collaboration in an integrated environment and reduce the time and cost of managing disparate systems and tools.

- Turn open-source and ecosystem investments into innovation opportunities with enterprise-ready, secure data lakes.

- Provide significant cost savings.

Lakehouses can:

- Reuse the data lake for 360-degree customer and operational intelligence, governance, and risk and compliance reporting.

- Ingest and integrate with transactional, operational, and analytical data to promote a complete insight.

- Extend information architectures to provide the right data at the right time on a common foundation for staging, storage, and access.

- Build and maintain a data foundation that powers data cataloging, curation, exploration, and discovery needs.

- Take a hybrid approach to access any data from any location, spanning real-time data to databases containing years of records.

- Integrate and expand analytics across multiple data repositories, revealing deeper, more holistic insights to help drive broader innovation and optimization across the enterprise to meet business needs ("at scale").

As organizations continue to move parts of their data estates and processing into hybrid multi-clouds, data lakes and lakehouses help provide optimum value, building on the following principles:

- Secure data-sharing across multiple teams accessing enterprise data: Organizations should be able to rely on data lake governance that houses raw structured and unstructured data—trusted, secured, and governed— with automated privacy and security anywhere.

- Presence of data-integration tools that combine data from disparate sources into valuable data sets: Such tools include those that provide extract, transform, load (ETL) function; enable controlled data replication and data virtualization (creating an integrated view of data spread across different data repositories, regardless of how they are physically stored and represented); and can extract large volumes of data from source systems and load it where applicable to a data warehouse.

- Via data virtualization, the ability to query data directly in the data lake without duplication or movement

In summary, a lakehouse is an emerging data-management architecture that converges data warehouse and data lake capabilities to meet modern data challenges such as ballooning costs, data silos, rapid data growth, and sprawling data, which otherwise often prevent organizations from getting the most out of their data. A lakehouse architecture is designed to help legacy warehouse customers tackle new problems and workloads by handling larger and more varied data sets, leading to new decision-making capabilities. The lakehouse architecture, if implemented correctly, can help reduce the need for complex data pipelines by enabling different analytic engines to operate on the same data store. These new abilities will ultimately help customers reduce the time needed to generate insights and optimize costs.

2

UNDERSTANDING THE LAKEHOUSE

A Lakehouse Analogy

Most people reading this book have been to a busy restaurant. You look around and see that the place is packed, yet everyone is getting their orders on time— whether they're seated for dining in or picking up food to deliver or take out. Think about the logistics that go into running a restaurant, coordinating all the steps of turning raw ingredients into delicious meals.

In a commercial kitchen, there are concurrently existing raw ingredients, sometimes raw meals, alcoholic and nonalcoholic beverages, and cooking equipment in use. Meanwhile, deliveries of kitchen and dining supplies by trucks to the loading dock on large pallets are taking place. That's the easy part. The palettes have to be unwrapped and processed. Each of the beverages, ingredients, and other restaurant supplies must be sorted, labeled, cataloged in the stock system, and routed to the correct storage areas. Some dry goods items may need to be stored in a pantry. Perishable items may need to be stored in large walk-in fridges and freezers.

It's important for kitchen staff to know when ingredients expire so the ones with the earliest expiration dates are used first. Certain ingredients need to be separated from one another to avoid cross-contamination, and different ingredients need to be stored at different temperatures for food safety and customer satisfaction. All of this needs to be accomplished as efficiently as possible to minimize food waste and spoilage.

When a customer orders a meal from the menu, the chef may need to tailor or modify each course. The meal choices are given to the kitchen staff, who prepare each course with attention to using the necessary ingredients, ensuring proper presentation of the food, and successfully timing delivery of each course. Without standardized processes, the kitchen staff can't really do their job effectively or safely. They would be spending more of their time looking for ingredients and less time cooking, delaying service to their customers. If the quality of the experience does not meet the guests' expectations, those guests might not return and may even write a bad review.

Preparing data requires a similar process. Similar concerns exist within data architectures of organizations. An organization will have all sorts of different data arriving at different times, in different volumes, from different sources—such as operational applications, external feeds, social media data, transactional data—and likely in a mix of structured, unstructured, and semi-structured data formats. All the different data needs to be collected, organized, and analyzed wherever it makes greatest business sense to do so. Raw data needs to be transformed into trusted insights that meet the expectations of customers. Like cooks in the kitchen, AI data engineers and data scientists need to be able understand the nuances of data and manipulate it so that ML models can be built, tested, trained, and deployed to meet the needs of both technical and business consumers.

Organizations need a place to dump all different types of data quickly and efficiently in different formats for later use. Data lakes can provide this capability cheaply and quickly by capturing raw structured, unstructured, and semi-structured data. Just as in the kitchen example, these raw ingredients need to be organized and transformed into something that's usable and trustworthy and that provides insights and analytics for the businesses to act upon. This is where enterprise data warehouses provide value. They can load data, sometimes from a data lake but also from other sources such as operational applications, which is then optimized and organized to let specific analytical tasks run against it. These tasks may include powering different BI workloads, such as building dashboards and reports, or the data could be fed into other analytical tools. Just like the ingredients and supplies in the pantries, freezers, and wine cellars, the data in the warehouse must be organized, cleansed, governed, and produced in a form that can be trusted for integrity.

While data lakes are valuable in capturing masses of data in a cost-effective way, the same data governance and data quality processes need to be applied to avoid these data lakes becoming "data swamps." Swamps can happen when there's a lot of duplicated, inaccurate, or incomplete data, which makes it difficult to track and manage assets. When the data becomes stale (has passed its sell-by or use-by date), it loses value when using it to try to create insights— the same way that ingredients can go bad over time in a restaurant. Data lakes also have challenges with query performance because they're neither built nor optimized to handle complex analytical queries. It can be challenging to extract insights out of lakes directly.

In contrast, a data warehouse provides fast and efficient query performance, although it can come at a high cost (just like those big freezers can be very costly to run), and organizations can't put everything into a data warehouse. While data warehouses can be better optimized to maintain data governance and quality, they offer limited support for semi-structured and unstructured data sources. Applications may require the freshest data, which might not be available in a data warehouse, because it takes time to sort, cleanse, and load data into it.

The Lakehouse: Unifying the Best of Both Worlds

Vendors have attempted to create the best of both worlds—data lakes and data warehouses—by combining them into the new technology of the lakehouse. This architecture is designed to provide the flexibility and cost effectiveness of a data lake with the performance and structure of a data warehouse. The lakehouse enables organizations to store data from the exploding number of new sources in a low-cost way and leverage built-in data management and governance capabilities, enabling organizations to power both BI and high-performance ML workloads efficiently and effectively.

If implemented correctly, organizations should be able to leverage their current investments in data lakes and data warehouses by adopting and implementing a lakehouse architecture and lakehouse technologies to help modernize their existing data lakes. Enterprises can also complement their data warehouses to support some of these new types of AI- and ML-driven workloads.

Much of this data is often distributed across many disparate silos, making it difficult to integrate and access. Data is represented in many different and sometimes complex formats as the market looks to support new paradigms and more diverse use cases that leverage unstructured and semi-structured data. A lot of time is spent transforming, cleansing, and integrating data. Data lakes represent a way to store massive amounts of different data using cheap commoditized hardware and storage via Hadoop, HDFS, or Hive. However, organizations' enthusiasm can wear off as soon as they find it difficult to manage and to get a good return on their data lake investment or even rely on the data (partly due to poor-quality data). Poor-quality data continues to plague most organizations like a virus. Once poor-quality data is shared across multiple business units and decisions have been made based on that data, it can be a difficult, costly, and lengthy process to recover from that mistake.

Data warehouses can be considered as the first iteration of tools to support analytics, enabling organizations to analyze data and make decisions at scale. Data warehouses enabled organizations to look back at historical data, starting with maybe a six-month window, then a year, then longer, as processing and computing power became more accessible and affordable. Over time, as volumes continued to grow, it became more challenging to store and retain all the data in a data warehouse. Additionally, organizations may have only a few years' worth of data or only a small slice of the operational data currently stored in their warehouses.

Organizations recognize that large volumes of unstructured data, even if not suitable for data warehouses, also contains great value—if it can be extracted. Unfortunately, when trying to analyze data that can be of poor quality, it can also be that the tools and analytical engines used to analyze the content in data lakes might not be as performant as those used for data warehouses. Many data lakes became more like data swamps with data becoming stale, difficult to maintain, and therefore untrustworthy. The need to scale compute and storage presents two different sets of needs across data lakes and data warehouses.

Data lakes and data warehouses each provide their own set of capabilities. When combined, scaling and governance can become key challenges, as data lakes and warehouses are designed for different purposes. The market evolved toward cloud-based data warehouses, which offer separation of computing and storage. Technologies such as Red Hat OpenShift, Red Hat Ceph Storage, Amazon S3, and other warehouse engines help solve the problem, making storage and computing inexpensive, readily available, and easier to manage and scale. Compute and storage need to be elastic, able to scale on demand when needed so that organizations are charged only for what they have used over the billable period.

A lakehouse, as shown in Figure 2.1, attempts to bridge these worlds by combining the best of both into one architecture. That said, these first-generation lakehouses have constraints that limit their ability to address cost and complexity challenges, such as these:

- Single-query engines are set up to support limited workloads, typically just for BI and ML.

- Lakehouses are typically deployed only over the cloud, with no support for hybrid multi-cloud deployments.

- Lakehouses offer minimal governance and metadata capabilities to deploy across an entire ecosystem.

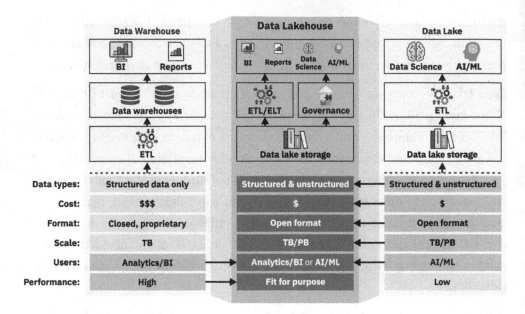

Figure 2.1: Lakehouses try to combine the best of data warehouses and data lakes

The Journey Continues: A Modern-Day Ladder for AI

What has been learned through history is that all the data paradigms discussed in the first chapter are cumulative. They don't simply go away or get replaced by the next paradigm. They must coexist. As these technologies mature, organizations recognize the value each provides at performing certain tasks.

What IBM has learned from countless data and AI projects is that every step of an organization's data or AI journey is critical. AI is not magic; it requires a thoughtful and well-architected approach. For example, most AI failures are due to problems in data preparation and data organization, not the AI models themselves. Success with AI models depends on achieving success first with how the data is collected and organized.

An AI Ladder, shown in Figure 2.2, represents a prescriptive approach to help customers overcome data challenges and accelerate their journey to AI, no matter where they currently are on their journey. It enables them to simplify and automate how an organization turns data into insights by unifying the collection, organization, and analysis of data, regardless of where it lives. By climbing the ladder to AI, enterprises can build a governed, efficient, agile, and future-proof approach to AI.

This original AI Ladder has four steps (often referred to as "rungs"):

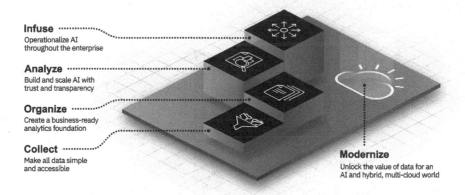

Figure 2.2: Four steps of the original AI Ladder

1. **Collect: Make data simple and accessible.** Collect data of every type, regardless of where it lives, enabling flexibility in the face of ever-changing data sources. Note that "collect" does not mean put data all in one place. In fact, quite the opposite. It means virtualizing the data, enabling access to wherever it lives as if it were consolidated.

2. **Organize: Create a business-ready analytics foundation.** Organize collected data into a trusted, business-ready foundation with built-in governance, protection, and compliance.

3. **Analyze: Build and scale AI with trust and transparency.** Analyze data in automated ways and benefit from AI models that empower teams to gain new insights and make better, smarter decisions.

4. **Infuse: Operationalize AI throughout the business.** Infuse AI throughout the business (across multiple departments and within various processes), drawing on predictions, automation, and optimization.

This ladder served its purpose as organizations began to adopt and leverage AI. Today, those same organizations are taking more of an "AI first" approach. They still need to collect, organize, analyze, and manage the growth of their data estates, but now they also need to add AI to their applications, automate workflows, replace/update existing workflows in line with new business processes and legislation, and let AI do the work, as shown in this modern AI Ladder in Figure 2.3.

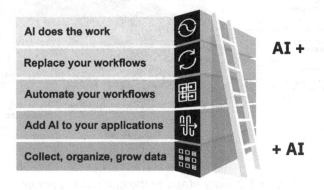

Figure 2.3: AI First, a modern-day ladder for AI

3

AI, DATA, AND GOVERNANCE—UNIFIED

AI, data, and governance are dependent on each other. None of these can successfully operate without the other.

AI depends on data as its life source. That data must be of the right quality and should be accessed securely only by those who have a business need for it. Data needs to be managed and analyzed using AI, and governance needs AI to continuously learn about potential threats and human behaviors and to comply with regulatory standards and legislation.

Consider one without the other, and an organization is more likely to fail.

This is precisely why IBM designed IBM watsonx. This AI and data platform is designed to enable enterprises to scale and accelerate the impact of the most advanced AI with trusted data. Organizations turning to AI today need access to a full technology stack that enables them to train, tune, and deploy AI models, including foundation models (explained below) and ML capabilities, across their organization with trusted data, speed, and governance—all in one place and designed to run across any cloud environment.

Unlike traditional machine learning, where each new use case requires a new model to be designed and built using specific data, foundation models are trained on large amounts of unlabeled data (data that does not have its characteristics, properties, or classifications tagged with it), which can then be adapted to new scenarios and business applications. A foundation model can therefore make massive AI scalability possible while amortizing the initial work of model building each time it is used because the data requirements for fine-tuning additional models are much lower. This can result in both increased ROI and much faster time to market.

Foundation models can be the basis for many applications of the AI model. Using self-supervised learning (defined by its use of labeled data sets to train algorithms that classify data or predict outcomes accurately) and fine-tuning, the model can apply general information it has learned to a specific task.

IBM watsonx offers businesses an AI development studio with access to IBM-curated and -trained foundation and open-source models, access to a data store that enables the gathering and cleansing of training and tuning data, and a toolkit for governance of AI in order to provide a seamless end-to-end AI workflow and make AI easier to adapt and scale.

Foundation models make deploying AI significantly more scalable, affordable, and efficient. IBM watsonx was built to meet the needs of enterprises so that clients can be more than just users; they can become AI-advantaged. IBM watsonx enables organizations to accelerate the training and deployment of custom AI capabilities across their entire business while retaining full control and governance of their data. IBM believes that there won't be "one model to rule them all," but rather different models tuned in different ways for specific use cases—models for language, geospatial imagery, code, chemistry, and many other modalities, as shown in Figure 3.1.

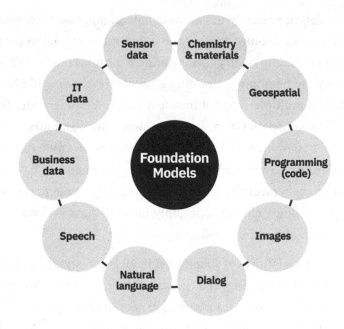

Figure 3.1: Foundation models cover a wide range of specific use cases

The Need for Foundation Models

Think about the data that exists in every business around the world. Whether it's sensor data, images, speech, different data about the business—this is all intelligence that's just waiting to be exploited. This reality drives the work that IBM has been doing to understand the foundation models that IBM should be building to help clients differentiate themselves from their competition.

A foundation model that is trained on large amounts of unlabeled data can then be adapted to new scenarios and use cases. Although a foundation model also requires a significant investment up front, it amortizes the initial work of AI model building each time it's used, as the data requirements for fine-tuning additional models built on the foundation model are significantly lower (we estimate 10x–100x). This could lead to both a huge increase in ROI and much faster time to deployment.

Foundation models are already the norm in natural language processing (NLP), where a single prompt can instruct a generative model to perform a new task, from producing poetry to answering a customer-service query. But language is only the beginning. Building a set of domain-specific foundation models trained on multiple types of business data (including code, time-series data, tabular data, geospatial data, semi-structured data, and mixed-modality data, such as text combined with images) can offer more value to businesses. These models can empower applications, ranging from code creation to drug discovery to cybersecurity, and will dramatically impact how people interact with technology, changing not only how business is done, but how organizations think about their business.

The flexibility and scalability of foundation models can significantly accelerate AI adoption. Instead of treating AI as a tactical "add on," enterprises are now empowered to put AI to work at the strategic core of their business. IBM, for example, expects foundation models to power about a third of AI within enterprise environments. In early work applying foundation models with clients, IBM has watched clients' time to value (the time it takes to get value from a service or product) become 70 percent faster than with a traditional AI approach.

Some types of foundation model technologies are as follows:

- **Foundation models** are built using a specific kind of neural-network architecture, called a transformer, which is designed to generate sequences of related data elements (for example, a sentence).

- The **transformer model** is a neural-network architecture useful for understanding language; it does not have to understand words one at a time but can instead look at an entire sentence at once for context and disambiguation. A technique called "self-attention" enables these models to focus on the particular words that are important in understanding the meaning of the sentence. Transformers single-handedly spawned the world of foundation models, and its birthplace research paper (https://proceedings.neurips.cc/paper_files/paper/2017/file/3f5ee243547dee91fbd053c1c4a845aa-Paper.pdf) spawned the AI inflection point that is happening today. AI transformer models can be encoder models (like Bidirectional Encoder Representations, or BERT), decoder models (like Generative Pre-Trained Transformers, or GPT), or encoder and decoder models (like T5). (Encoders are designed to learn embeddings that can be used for various predictive modeling tasks such as classification. In contrast, decoders are designed to generate new texts—for example, answering user queries.)

- **Neural networks** are a set of algorithms modeled loosely after the neural networks found in the human brain. They are designed to recognize hidden patterns in data.

- An **algorithm** is a procedure used for solving a problem or performing a computation. Algorithms act as an exact list of instructions that conduct a sequence of specified actions in either hardware- or software-based routines.

- **Generative AI** refers to a set of AI algorithms that can generate new outputs—such as text, images, code, or audio—based on the training data, unlike traditional AI systems that are designed to recognize patterns and make predictions. Sometimes the AI that powers these solutions are referred to as decoders.

- **Natural language processing (NLP)** is the technology that gives computers the ability to understand text and spoken words in much the same way human beings can. NLP combines computational linguistics (rule-based modeling of human language) with statistical, machine-learning, and deep-learning models. These technologies enable computers to process human language in the form of text or "voice data" and to "understand" its full meaning, complete with the speaker's or writer's intent and sentiment.

- **Machine learning (ML)** refers to a broad set of techniques to train a computer to learn from its inputs, using existing data and one or more "training" methods, instead of being explicitly programmed. ML helps a computer to achieve AI.

- **Deep learning (DL)** is a technique for implementing ML that relies on deep artificial neural networks to perform complex tasks such as image recognition, object detection, and NLP. The "deep" in DL refers to a neural network composed of more than three layers (which include the input and the output layers).

- **Geospatial data** includes information related to locations on the earth's surface, such as latitude and longitude coordinates and addresses. These factors go through a secondary process to assist in representing them on a map.

IBM continues to develop a set of foundation models for business, which includes large language models (LLMs), IT automation models, digital labor models, cybersecurity models, and many more to come.

Recognizing that one size doesn't fit all, IBM offers a family of language and code foundation models of different sizes and architectures. Each model family has a geology-themed code name—Granite, Sandstone, Obsidian, Slate, and Moonstone—and brings together cutting-edge innovations from IBM Research and the open research community. Each model can be customized for a range of enterprise tasks.

- **Granite** models are based on a decoder-only, GPT-like architecture for generative tasks.

- **Sandstone** models use an encoder-decoder architecture and are well suited for fine-tuning on specific tasks (interchangeable with Google's popular T5 models).

- **Obsidian** models use a new modular architecture developed by IBM Research, providing high inference efficiency and levels of performance across a variety of tasks.

- **Slate** refers to a family of encoder-only (RoBERTa-based) models, which, while not generative, are fast and effective for many enterprise NLP tasks.

- **Moonstone** refers to a novel architecture based on dense associative memory, which stores and reliably retrieves many more patterns than the number of neurons in the network.

When a business decides it wants to go to work on AI, it has three choices with IBM:

- It can build its own models—and many clients and partners will want to do that—and IBM watsonx provides the capability for that.

- Some organizations may want to use open-source models, other models, IBM models, or a combination. With IBM watsonx, they can. The IBM partnership with Hugging Face includes open-source models in its workbench.

- Some organizations might want to just use the IBM foundation models to get results.

Regardless of the approach an organization chooses, IBM will help the company experiment with it, do the model-tuning, build and evaluate the model, and deploy (and maintain) a tuned model on any cloud. This aligns to the IBM strategy around hybrid cloud and AI.

All IBM watsonx models are trained on IBM's curated, enterprise-focused lakehouse on the custom-designed, cloud-native AI supercomputer named Vela.

Efficiency and sustainability are core design principles for watsonx. IBM Research invented new technologies for efficient model training, including the LiGO algorithm that recycles small models and "grows" them into larger ones. This method can save from 40 to 70 percent of the time, cost, and carbon output required to train a model. More information on LiGO is available at the Massachusetts Institute of Technology news pages here: https://news.mit.edu/2023/new-technique-machine-learning-models-0322.

To improve inference speeds, IBM leverages its deep expertise in "quantization," which is a way of shrinking models from 32-point floating-point arithmetic to much smaller integer-bit formats. Reducing AI model precision can result in huge efficiency benefits without sacrificing accuracy. IBM hopes to run these compressed models on its AI-optimized chip IBM AIU, used in the cloud-native AI supercomputer Vela, which is designed to run and train deep-learning models faster and more efficiently than a general-purpose CPU. More information on quantization and IBM AIU is available at https://research.ibm.com/blog/ibm-artificial-intelligence-unit-aiu.

With watsonx, users have access to the toolset, technology, infrastructure, and consulting expertise to build their own or fine-tune and adapt available AI models on their own data and deploy them at scale in a trustworthy and open environment. Competitive differentiation and unique business value will be able to be increasingly derived from how adaptable an AI model can be to an enterprise's unique data and domain knowledge.

The IBM watsonx platform consists of three unique product sets to help address these needs, as shown in Figure 3.2:

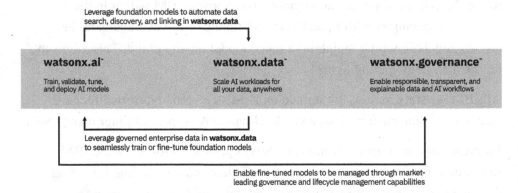

Figure 3.2: Scale and accelerate the impact of AI with trusted data using IBM watsonx

As a platform, watsonx is represented in Figure 3.3.

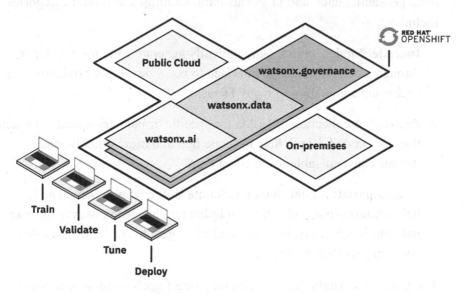

Figure 3.3: IBM watsonx conceptual architecture

IBM watsonx.ai

This is a next-generation enterprise studio for AI builders to train, validate (test), tune, and deploy both traditional ML and new generative AI capabilities powered by foundation models via an open and intuitive user interface.

- The AI studio provides a range of foundation models, training and tuning tools, and a cost-effective infrastructure that facilitates the entire data and AI lifecycle, from data preparation through model development, deployment, and monitoring.

- The studio also includes a foundation model library that gives users easy access to IBM-curated and -trained foundation models. As mentioned previously, foundation models use a large, curated set of enterprise data, backed by a robust filtering and cleansing process and with an auditable data lineage. These models are being trained not only on language, but on a variety of modalities, including code, time-series data, tabular data, geospatial data, and IT events data. Examples of model categories include:

○ **fm.code:** Models built to automatically generate code for developers through a natural-language interface to boost developer productivity and enable the automation of many IT tasks

○ **fm.NLP:** A collection of LLMs for specific or industry-specific domains that use curated data to help mitigate bias and more quickly make domains customizable using client data

○ **fm.geospatial:** Models built on climate and remote sensing data to help organizations understand and plan for changes in natural disaster patterns, biodiversity, land use, and other geophysical processes that could impact their businesses

• The watsonx.ai studio builds upon Hugging Face's open-source libraries and offers thousands of Hugging Face open models and data sets. This is part of IBM's commitment to delivering an open ecosystem approach that enables users to leverage the best models and architecture for their unique business needs.

IBM watsonx.data

This is a fit-for-purpose data store built on an open-lakehouse architecture that is optimized for governed data and AI workloads, supported by querying, governance, and open data formats to access and share data.

• The solution can manage workloads both on premises and across hybrid multi-cloud environments while leveraging internal and external data sets.

• Through workload optimization, with this solution an organization can reduce data warehouse costs by up to 50 percent. This is based on comparing published 2023 list prices normalized for virtual private cloud hours of watsonx.data to several major cloud data warehouse vendors. Savings may vary depending on configurations, workloads, and vendors.

- It enables users to access robust data through a single point of entry while applying multiple fit-for-purpose query engines to uncover valuable insights.

- It also provides built-in governance tools, automation, and integration with an organization's existing databases and tools to simplify setup and user experience.

IBM watsonx.governance

This AI governance toolkit enables trusted AI workflows. The solution helps organizations:

- Operationalize governance to help mitigate the risk, time, and cost associated with manual processes. It also provides the documentation necessary to drive transparent and explainable outcomes.

- Provide the mechanisms to protect customer privacy, proactively detect model bias and drift, and meet the organization's ethics standards.

- Meet existing and future compliance needs, such as the EU's Digital Services Act and Digital Markets Act (find details online at https://en.wikipedia.org/wiki/Digital_Services_Act and https://en.wikipedia.org/wiki/Digital_Markets_Act)

With the watsonx platform, organizations are able to meet their needs in five key business areas: interacting and conversing with customers and employees, automating business workflows and internal processes, automating IT processes, protecting against threats, and tackling sustainability goals.

IBM watsonx.ai foundation models are fused within all IBM major software products, including these:

- **IBM watsonx Code Assistant:** This solution taps generative AI to help developers generate code with a straightforward English language command.

- **AIOps Insights:** This product delivers AI Operations (AIOps) capabilities enhanced with foundation models expected for code and NLP to provide greater visibility into performance across IT environments, helping IT operations (ITOps) managers and Site Reliability Engineers (SREs) resolve incidents in a more expedient and cost-efficient way.

- **IBM watsonx Assistant and watsonx Orchestrate:** IBM's digital labor products are expected to be combined with an NLP foundation model to enable enhanced employee productivity and customer service experiences. (Digital labor is a form of labor characterized by the production of value through interaction with information and communication technologies, such as digital platforms or AI).

- **Environmental Intelligence Suite (EIS):** IBM EIS Builder Edition is planned to be enabled by the geospatial foundation model and available in preview later this year, enabling organizations to create tailored solutions that address and mitigate environmental risks based on their unique goals and needs.

Data Fabric Capabilities

The IBM watsonx platform leverages and is built upon existing IBM Cloud Pak technologies, which in turn sit upon Red Hat OpenShift, Enterprise Linux, and Ansible Automation Platform, providing the platform's hybrid cloud capabilities as shown in Figure 3.4.

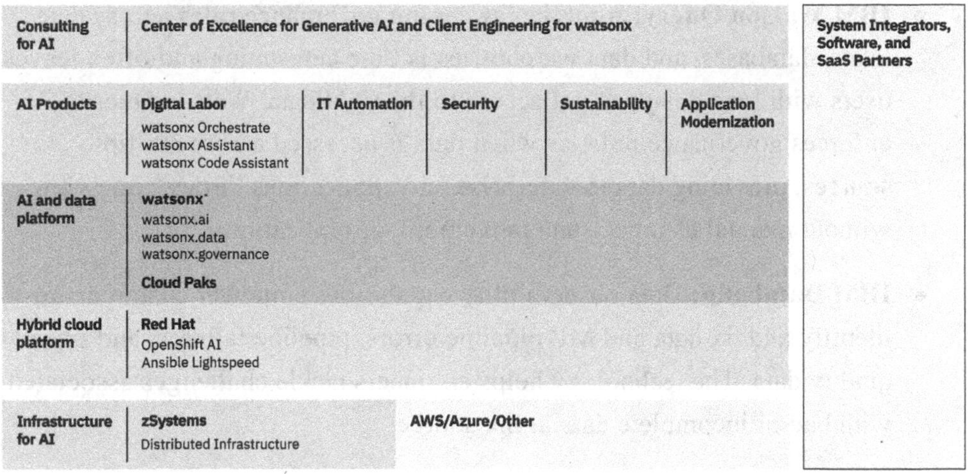

Consulting for AI	Center of Excellence for Generative AI and Client Engineering for watsonx					System Integrators, Software, and SaaS Partners
AI Products	**Digital Labor** watsonx Orchestrate watsonx Assistant watsonx Code Assistant	**IT Automation**	**Security**	**Sustainability**	**Application Modernization**	
AI and data platform	**watsonx˚** watsonx.ai watsonx.data watsonx.governance **Cloud Paks**					
Hybrid cloud platform	**Red Hat** OpenShift AI Ansible Lightspeed					
Infrastructure for AI	**zSystems** Distributed Infrastructure		**AWS/Azure/Other**			

Figure 3.4: IBM watsonx leverages Cloud Pak technologies

IBM Cloud Pak for Data was designed to deliver a set of data-fabric capabilities to help predict outcomes faster and enable organizations to collect, organize, and analyze data, no matter where it may reside. The platform thus helps to improve productivity and reduce complexity by building a data fabric that connects siloed data distributed across a hybrid cloud landscape. It leverages key services and capabilities, including these:

- **IBM Knowledge Catalog:** This catalog enables intelligent governance across a hybrid distributed data landscape through advanced data discovery, data quality management, automated data lineage, data cataloging, and data protection capabilities. The solution is powered by active metadata and is designed to enable self-service access to trusted data for insights generation as well as for regulatory compliance use cases. Access, curate, categorize, and share data, knowledge assets, and their relationships, wherever they reside. Also, integration between MANTA's end-to-end Data Lineage platform and IBM Knowledge Catalog's business-friendly native data lineage provides a more complete picture of technical, historical, and indirect data lineage.

- **IBM Watson Query:** Applying sweeping governance rules across data lakes, databases, and data warehouses is time consuming and often leaves users with long delays to get access to the right data. Watson Query enforces governance policies when data is accessed across multiple sources, providing data to enterprise end applications through one view without manual changes, data movement, or replication.

- **IBM Databand:** Data observability capabilities empower customers to identify and fix data and ML pipeline errors, pipeline failures, and poor-quality data. The technology helps engineers tackle challenges associated with bad or incomplete data at the source.

- **IBM Match 360 with Watson:** This tool helps consolidate data from disparate sources across domains and systems to provide a broad view of persons, organizations, and custom entities. This is done with the assistance of ML and governance capabilities to provide a simplified experience for business users.

- **IBM Security Guardium Insights:** With out-of-the-box compliance capabilities and workflows such as compliance policy creation, audit process definition, access privilege assignment, and user activity reports, IBM Security Guardium Insights helps the enterprise quickly meet its data regulatory needs. Its robust capabilities help enterprises build and automate compliance policy enforcement and stream and centralize data activity across a hybrid-cloud ecosystem. Guardium Insights is designed to provide data security specialists with features such as automated compliance, auditing and reporting, and real-time monitoring.

In the next chapter, we take an in-depth look at watsonx.data, which offers a comprehensive solution with a set of capabilities designed to optimize different workloads across a wide range of data sets.

4

A Different Kind of Lakehouse:
watsonx.data

A combination of on-premises and cloud-native warehouses and custom data lakes is common for enterprise architecture today, as shown in Figure 4.1. Juggling costs, siloed data, and data governance are constant challenges.

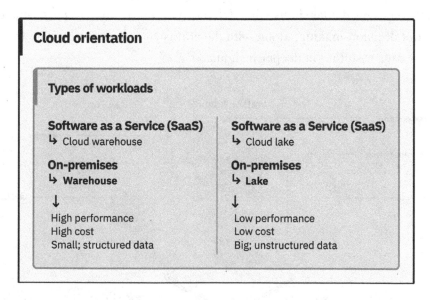

Figure 4.1: On-premises, cloud-native warehouses and custom data lakes commonly found in today's enterprise architectures

As stated in an earlier chapter, the lakehouse is an emerging architecture that offers the low cost and flexibility of a data lake with the performance and structure of a data warehouse. Most lakehouse solutions offer a high-performance query engine over low-cost storage in conjunction with a metadata governance layer. Intelligent metadata layers make it easier for users to categorize and classify unstructured data (such as video and voice) and semi-structured data (such as eXtensible Markup Language (XML), JavaScript Object Notation (JSON), and emails). In a perfect world, a lakehouse will offer open-source technologies that reduce data duplication and simplify complex Extract, Transform, Load (ETL) pipelines. Be aware that some first-generation lakehouses have key constraints that limit their ability to address the challenges of cost and complexity. For example, a single-query engine that's designed for BI or ML workloads could well be ineffective when it's used for another workload type.

Every workload is unique and should be optimized with the best-suited environment to keep cost at a minimum and performance at a maximum. Organizations need a lakehouse that delivers an optimal level of performance for better decision-making, along with the ability to unlock more value from all types of data, resulting in deeper insights.

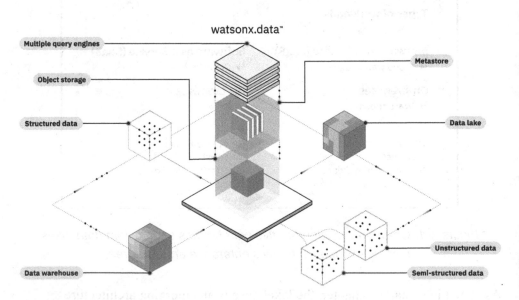

Figure 4.2: IBM watsonx.data concepts architecture

IBM watsonx.data is an open, hybrid, governed data store optimized for all data, analytics, and AI workloads, conceptualized as shown in Figure 4.2. IBM watsonx.data is designed to help organizations:

- **Access all their data** and maximize workload coverage across all hybrid-cloud environments. Expect seamless deployment of a fully managed service across any cloud or on-premises environment. Access any data source, wherever it resides, through a single point of entry and combine it using open data formats. Integrate into existing environments with open source, open standards, and interoperability with IBM and third-party services.

- **Accelerate time** to trusted insights. Start with built-in governance and automation; strengthen enterprise compliance and security with unified governance across the entire ecosystem. A click-and-go console helps teams ingest, access, and transform data and run workloads. The product provides a dashboard that makes it easier for organizations to save money and deliver fresh, trusted insights.

- **Reduce the cost** of a data warehouse by up to 50 percent via workload optimization across multiple query engines and storage tiers. Optimize costly warehouse workloads with fit-for-purpose engines that scale up and down automatically. Reduce costs by eliminating duplication of data when the enterprise uses low-cost object storage; extract more value from the data in ineffective data lakes. This cost reduction was calculated by comparing published 2023 list prices normalized for virtual private cloud (VPC) hours of IBM watsonx.data to several major cloud data warehouse vendors. Savings may vary depending on configurations, workloads, and vendors.

Through many consulting engagements, IBM has found that organizations are often at one or more of these stages:

- Remaining on traditional warehouse or analytic appliances but looking for ways to get greater flexibility and to also perhaps tackle new workloads

- Have adopted the traditional data lakes but are running into issues of getting sufficient return on their investment and having to manage those systems

- Have adopted the cloud data warehouses but are concerned with ever-increasing billing costs

All three of these groups are looking for ways to get more flexibility, adopt more workloads, reduce costs, and reduce complexity.

IBM watsonx.data is designed to address the needs of all three groups and the shortcomings of some first-generation lakehouses. It combines open, flexible, and low-cost storage of data lakes with the transactional qualities and performance of a data warehouse. This enables data (structured, semi-structured, and unstructured) to reside in commodity storage, bringing together the best of data lakes and warehouses to enable best-in-class AI, BI, and ML in one solution without vendor lock-in.

Some of the key capabilities of watsonx.data are:

- It scales for BI across all data with multiple high-performance query engines optimized for different workloads (for example: Presto, Spark, Db2, Netezza, etc.).

- It enables data-sharing between these different engines.

- It uses shared common data storage across data lake and data warehouse functions, avoiding unnecessary time-consuming ETL/ELT jobs.

- It eradicates unnecessary data duplication and replication.

- It provides consistent governance, security, and user experience across hybrid multi-clouds.

- It leverages an open and flexible architecture built on open source without vendor lock-in.

- It can be deployed across hybrid-cloud environments (on-premises, private, public clouds) on multiple hyperscalers.

- It offers a wide range of prebuilt integration capabilities incorporating IBM data-fabric capabilities.

- It provides global governance across all data in the enterprise, leveraging the IBM data-fabric capabilities.

- It is extensible through APIs, value-add partner ecosystems, accelerators, and third-party solutions.

- It offers organizations the flexibility of starting their lakehouse implementation standalone and later expanding to the IBM Cloud Pak for Data platform configuration as shown in Figure 4.3.

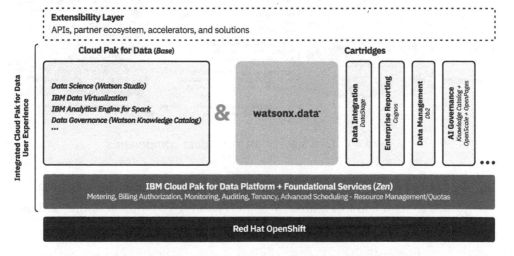

Figure 4.3: watsonx integrated with IBM Cloud Pak for Data

Modularity and flexibility are key when implementing a lakehouse. If an organization has a Hadoop data lake with data stored on Hadoop Distributed

File System (HDFS), the metadata can be cataloged using Hive, and the metadata and data can be brought to the lakehouse (watsonx.data) so that, from day one, the most appropriate engines can be used to query the data. New data arriving in the lakehouse needs to be integrated with existing data using the metadata and storage layers (Hive and HDFS) and continuously analyzed without affecting existing applications using the data lake. Over time, data can be moved into the data lake at an organization's own pace.

Many of the watsonx.data components shown in Figure 4.4 are based on open-source technologies such as Presto, Iceberg, Hive, Ranger, and others. IBM watsonx.data also offers a wide range of integration with existing IBM and third-party products.

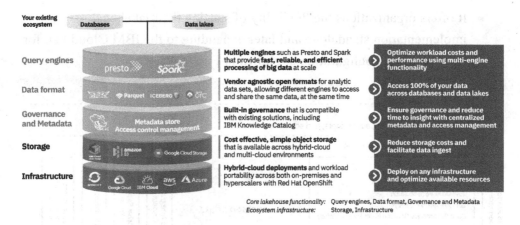

Figure 4.4: Overview of watsonx.data components

IBM watsonx.data can be deployed across multiple environments, including but not limited to IBM Cloud, Amazon Web Services (AWS) infrastructure, and on premises.

The storage layer is centered around object storage, which is highly available, highly scalable, and inexpensive.

A governance and metadata layer integrates existing Netezza and Db2 services to achieve metadata sharing using open-data formats such as Parquet, ORC, and

Avro (a serialization format for record data and for streaming data pipelines) and leverages the Apache Iceberg table format. It uses multiple engines, such as Presto and Spark, which provide fast, reliable, efficient processing of big data at scale. Let's take a look at each layer in more detail.

Infrastructure

From an infrastructure layer perspective (Figure 4.5), "quick start" steps enable organizations using Software as a Service (SaaS) tools to deploy in minutes, ready to bring and store their data into S3 object storage. Organizations may also choose to connect to existing data warehouses and look at the data using virtualization or federation techniques.

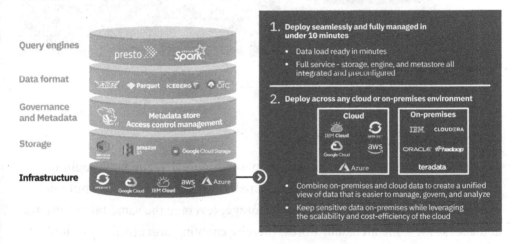

Figure 4.5: watsonx.data infrastructure layer

Storage and Data Formats

IBM watsonx.data is designed to leverage various storage solutions, such as Amazon S3, IBM Cloud, Google Cloud Storage, and HDFS. Apache Iceberg helps solve the problem of bringing structure to data lakes. It's a metadata file that sits with the data files so that, as changes are made to the data, it keeps track of those records. Think of it as appending to that metadata file. It provides certain atomicity, consistency, isolation, and durability (ACID) transactional guarantees and the ability to roll back in time for any audit purposes. Organizations can view and understand the transactions that occurred and their completion status by looking back in time at previous states. See Figure 4.6.

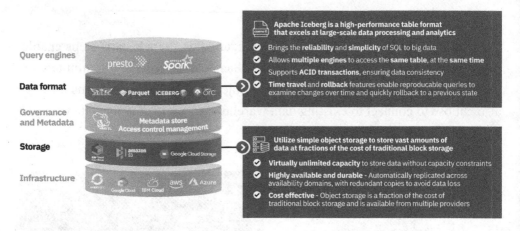

Figure 4.6: watsonx.data storage and data format layers

Governance and Metadata

The governance and metadata layer, shown in Figure 4.7, can be thought of as the glue that holds the multi-engine capabilities together. For example, it enables all engines to access the same storage, leverage the same table formats, and access the same metadata stores, thereby enabling organizations to look at the same sets of data through a unified catalog. Users are able to understand exactly what the data is, where it is, and what it looks like, no matter which query engine they are using. When a user changes or updates data in watsonx. data with an engine such as Presto, the metadata and catalog will be updated so that when that same user looks at that catalog later through a different query engine (for example, the Netezza engine), that user can continue exactly where they left off in watsonx.data.

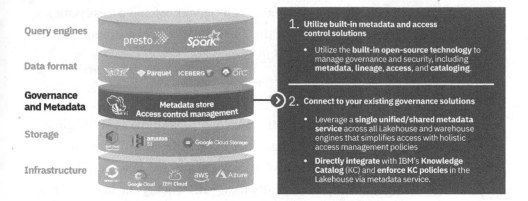

Figure 4.7: watsonx.data governance and metadata layer

Access-control management helps provide consistent governance across all watsonx.data lakehouse assets, integrating with IBM Knowledge Catalog capabilities to participate in global governance and providing a single source of the truth for policies and their enforcement. This is achieved through metadata integration and plug-ins to the engines.

There are three levels of user access controls in watsonx.data:

- **User Authentication (Level 1 access control):** watsonx.data works with a variety of Identity Provider Services, such as Identity Access Management (IAM) and Lightweight Directory Access Protocol (LDAP). Users who access the service through UIs, APIs, SQL editors, and command lines will be authenticated using their user ID and password, API keys, or authentication tokens.

- **User Access to resources (Level 2 access control):** Roles can be assigned for watsonx.data users to access lakehouse resources. Roles at this level include Viewer, Editor, and Administrator. Resources include Instances, Engines, Catalogs. Storage, and Databases.

- **User Access to data (Level 3 access control):** watsonx.data enables data administrators to define data access policies for deeper levels of governance. Access policies can be defined on schemas, tables, columns, and rows. Users are checked for access based on defined access policies. Advanced governance involving the masking of data, for example, leverages IBM Knowledge Catalog governance.

Querying

The querying layer, as previously mentioned, enables multiple query engines to coexist within watsonx.data. One size does not fit all when it comes to querying all the different types of data that may exist in a lakehouse. This layer enables the best engines to be intelligently assigned to query the target data sets for cost optimization of workloads. The different query engines are assigned infrastructure profiles. For example, Presto can leverage different flavors of worker nodes (used to run containerized applications and handle networking to ensure that traffic between applications across the cluster and from outside of the cluster can be properly facilitated). One node might be used to better manage CPU-dense tasks that require heavy computing of arcane encryption. Another might be cache-optimized to cope with large data scans or work with large amounts of data that need to be close to the engine. By scaling out the worker nodes, organizations can be assured they have a sufficient cache to handle the workloads. All engines can be ephemeral and elastic as well as be usage-based so organizations can use instances of these engines to run their workloads, pause them, or delete them at will. Organizations are billed for only what they use and when they use it, scaling up and down to meet the necessary service-level agreements (SLAs). See Figure 4.8.

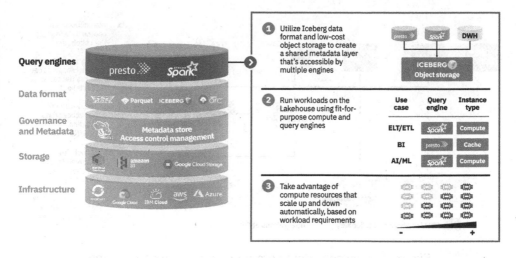

Figure 4.8: watsonx.data querying layer

IBM watsonx.data Core and Ecosystem Components

Figure 4.9 shows the core watsonx.data lakehouse components and the integrations across the IBM ecosystem. Both Db2 Warehouse and Netezza can access and work with data in watsonx.data via their compatibility with Iceberg tables. They work with object storage so that they can persist and read data directly from object storage. They integrate with the watsonx.data metadata service so that they don't have to recatalog any of the data they need to access or use in watsonx.data. For organizations with mainframes, the Data Gate service replicates data from Db2 on z/OS into the Db2 Warehouse, enabling that data to participate in the watsonx.data ecosystem.

IBM Knowledge Catalog integration provides the policies that the watsonx.data store needs to enforce on the data that it understands and owns. Hadoop and legacy data lakes can plug into this ecosystem.

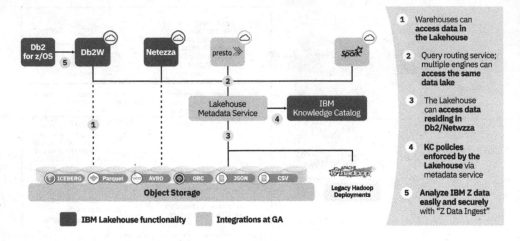

Figure 4.9: watsonx.data core and ecosystem components

A watsonx.data and watsonx.ai Integration Workflow Example

Let's work through a watsonx workflow that demonstrates how watsonx.data and watsonx.ai work together seamlessly. This example covers data acquisition, data cleansing, annotation, and filtering in watsonx.data, bridging seamlessly to tokenization and LLM training in watsonx.ai.

This example uses BluePile, a data corpus that is used to train all the IBM LLMs. A data pile (or corpus) is any collection of data and might be related to customer interactions captured over the phone or record logs from transactions. First, data acquisition is performed for the approved BluePile data sets. The workflow then follows a well-defined data-acquisition process to populate and grow the BluePile corpus from a variety of external and internal data sources. This process includes identifying and prioritizing specific data coverage needs, identifying relevant data sources to address those needs, evaluating potential risks, and implementing a governed and traceable series of risk-mitigation measures for each source. Figure 4.10 shows the high-level workflow and integration between watsonx.data and watsonx.ai.

watsonx.data + watsonx.ai workflow
Illustrated using Blue Pile - data corpus used in training IBM's Large Language Models (LLMs)

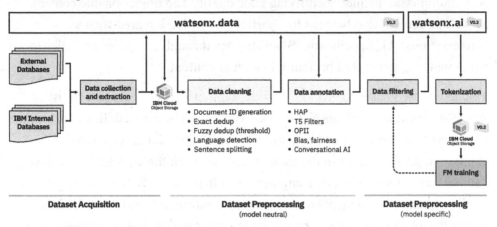

Figure 4.10: watsonx.data and watsonx.ai workflow and integration

To power this entire process, data downloaded into IBM BluePile is stored in the lakehouse with granular metadata that provides traceable provenance for each file or document in the corpus. IBM watsonx.data provides a state-of-the-art data management system to manage the acquisition and curation processes for BluePile. As a fit-for-purpose data store optimized for managing data and AI workloads, the lakehouse provides open data formats to access and share data across multiple engines and runtimes and uses familiar SQL-based querying to analyze and filter out unsuitable content. Using these features, a dashboard shows the BluePile composition, including the amount of data from each data source, sample examples, languages identified, and other statistics. The lakehouse also provides support for versioning and tagging, which enable full traceability.

Once the source data sets are in the lakehouse, the power of Spark integration and the ease of use of Jupyter Notebook is available to the data engineering team to perform data cleansing tasks at scale. These tasks include operations such as exact deduplication, fuzzy deduplication, language detection, and sentence splitting. During these processing steps, data is read from and written back into the lakehouse with the tagging function used to manage versioning.

Once data cleansing is completed, the workflow proceeds to data annotation. Annotation tasks include identifying poor-quality and objectionable content, as well as content that belongs to a particular application area such as conversational AI. Specifically, BluePile goes through extensive analytics to annotate hate, abuse, and profanity in textual content.

The lakehouse is able to quickly provide summaries and aggregate statistics across different annotations and data set versions. These capabilities enable data engineers to experiment and determine the right thresholds for removing hate, abuse, and profanities from the training corpus. With the enriched annotated data sets in watsonx.data, data engineers can then perform data filtering based on the training requirements desired for each individual model run. This is where the lakehouse support for versioning and tagging makes it seamless to manage and track the different choices and to work with the right subsets of data for model development. As an example, a version with less-aggressive filtering of unsavory content may be used for internal experimentation, another with more-aggressive filtering for production use, and yet another with the addition of proprietary data only for models to be consumed in products. Once again, filtered data sets are properly versioned along with threshold information and other policy choices.

Starting out to build a model from hundreds of terabytes can be a daunting task. IBM watsonx.data provides randomized samples of the content sources. Data engineers can perform analysis and analytics of these data samples to look for additional filters and determine how various preprocessing steps can be enhanced further before expanding to the full data sets. With this data having been filtered out based on model training requirements, data engineers are ready to use this data and start the model-training process.

This is where the watsonx.ai training and validation stack comes into play. Typically, this also implies the shift of responsibility from the data engineering and preprocessing team to the model development and data science team. The first step in training a model is to perform tokenization of the data according to model requirements. A token in this context is the most basic element of data. It could be a word in a sentence or part of a word. The tokenization is launched using Jupyter Notebook, which under the covers uses CodeFlare and Ray, part of the watsonx.ai training stack.

Before proceeding, here are explanations for the following terms:

- **CodeFlare** is an abstraction for developing, resource-scaling, queuing, and managing distributed AI/ML and Python workloads on the Red Hat OpenShift Container Platform.

- **Ray/KubeRay:** Ray is a unified framework for scaling AI and running distributed Python workloads. KubeRay is an open-source Kubernetes operator for deploying and managing Ray applications on Kubernetes.

- **TorchX** is a universal job launcher for PyTorch applications. TorchX is designed to have fast iteration time for training/research and support for end-to-end production ML pipelines.

- **PyTorch** is an AI framework for AI research and commercial production for machine learning and deep learning.

- **Multi-Cluster Application Dispatcher (MCAD)** is a Kubernetes controller providing mechanisms for applications to manage batch jobs in a single or multi-cluster environment.

To start the process of tokenizing the data, the user queries watsonx.data using the credentials (known as a "tag version ID") provided by the data processing team. This query will produce a copy of the data set and make it available in watsonx.data, which can be used by the tokenization jobs. Use of tag versions not only reduces friction between data processing and model training teams, but also maintains traceable provenance to the source for every single document used for training models. Once this model-specific training data set is available, the tokenization script is launched using CodeFlare APIs, which automate and abstract the process of invoking a cluster and the intricacies of deploying it in a multi-cloud environment. With CodeFlare, data scientists can simply focus on model training, not deployment.

Once the tokenization script has been launched, the Ray cluster is up and running and tokenization is underway. Once tokenization is completed, users are ready for the final step of foundation-model training. The CodeFlare SDK provides an easy interface for data scientists, while abstracting the details of the cluster management. Thanks to the tight integration between TorchX and MCAD—both of which are components of the watsonx.ai training stack—a simple Jupyter Notebook can be used to launch the training job. In this particular case, a Sandstone training job also launches. Once the command is issued, under-the-covers resources are procured by MCAD, training containers appear, and a distributed model-training job gets started by TorchX, all coordinated by the watsonx.ai training stack. At the end of the training process, a foundation model is ready to be deployed and leveraged using the watsonx.ai inference stack.

This walk-through hopefully illustrates how the watsonx platform provides a seamless experience for both data engineers and data scientists involved in the foundation-model development process. Built on an open hybrid platform, these capabilities are available via a simple Jupyter Notebook interface across a hybrid multi-cloud environment. This powerful combination of watsonx.data and watsonx.ai is being used to manage the development of all IBM LLMs with built-in governance and automation.

In the next chapter, we discuss the principles of both data governance and AI governance when implementing a lakehouse.

5

LAKEHOUSE AND GOVERNANCE

The term "governance" can be defined as "the process of making and enforcing decisions within an organization or society." For the purposes of the book, we will focus on data and AI governance.

Data Governance

Data governance is a key aspect of managing an organization's data assets. Ultimately, the goal of data governance is knowing where data assets and artefacts come from, what they are, who should have access to them, how they should be used, and how to manage their retention. Several key technology building blocks exist to meet the need to integrate and improve data privacy, access, quality, and traceability for all the data in an organization.

It's important to identify the business objectives, desired outcomes, key stakeholders, and data needed to deliver against these objectives. Technology and data architecture play a crucial role in enabling data governance and achieving these objectives.

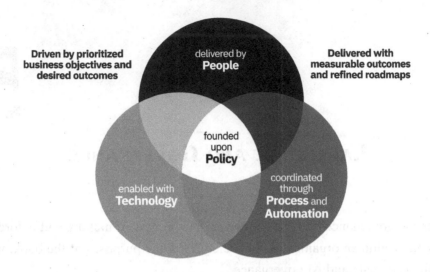

Figure 5.1: Data governance depends on people, technology, policy, and process

- **People** refers to the organizational structure, roles, and responsibilities of those involved in data governance, including those who own, collect, store, manage, and use the data.

- **Policy** provides the guidelines for using, protecting, and managing the data, ensuring consistency and compliance.

- **Process** refers to the procedures for communication, collaboration, and management of data, including data collection, storage, protection, and usage.

- **Technology** refers to the tools and systems used to support data governance, such as data management platforms and security solutions.

These intersect as shown in Figure 5.1. For example, if one of the goals is to improve customer retention, the data-governance program should focus on where and how customer data is produced and consumed across the organization, ensuring that the organization's customer data is accurate, complete, protected, and accessible to those who need it to make decisions that will improve customer retention.

It's important to coordinate and standardize policies, roles, and data management processes to align them with the business objectives. This will ensure that data is being used effectively and that all stakeholders are working toward the same goal.

Starting a data-governance program may seem like a daunting task, but by starting small and focusing on delivering prioritized business outcomes, data governance can become a natural extension of the day-to-day business as opposed to being treated as an ad hoc add-on.

Building a data-governance program is an iterative and incremental process that can include the following steps:

Step 1: Define a data strategy and data-governance goals and objectives.

An organization should consider both long-term strategic goals and short-term tactical goals and remember that goals may be influenced by external factors such as regulations and compliance.

A data strategy identifies, prioritizes, and aligns business objectives across an organization and its various lines of business. Across multiple business objectives, a data strategy will identify data needs, metrics, key performance indicators (KPIs), stakeholders, and required data management processes, technology priorities, and capabilities.

It's important to regularly review and update the data strategy as the business and priorities change. If an organization doesn't have a data strategy, it should build one and should include contributions from the appropriate business and technical stakeholders.

Once the organization has established a clear understanding of business objectives and data needs, the organization should set data-governance goals and priorities. For example, an effective data-governance program may:

- Improve data quality, which can lead to more accurate and reliable decision-making.
- Increase data security to protect sensitive information.

- Enable compliance and reporting against industry regulations.

- Improve overall trust and reliability of your data assets.

- Make data more accessible and usable, which can improve efficiency and productivity.

- Clearly define organizational goals and objectives that will guide the prioritization and development of a data-governance program, ultimately driving revenue, cost savings, and customer satisfaction.

Step 2: Secure executive and essential stakeholder support.

Identify key stakeholders and roles for the data-governance program and decide who will need to be involved in its execution. This should include employees, managers, IT staff, data architects, line-of-business owners, and data custodians within and outside the organization.

An executive sponsor is crucial. This individual should understand the significance and objectives of data governance, recognize the business value that data governance enables, and support the investment required to achieve these outcomes.

With key sponsorship in place, the next step is to assemble a team to understand the compelling narrative, define what needs to be accomplished, determine how to raise awareness, and decide how to build the funding model that will be used to support the implementation of the data-governance program.

By effectively engaging key stakeholders, as well as identifying and delivering clear business value, the implementation of a data-governance program can become a strategic advantage for the organization.

Step 3: Assess, build, and refine the data-governance program.

With business objectives understood and data-governance sponsors and stakeholders in place, it's important to map these objectives against the existing people, process, policy, and technology capabilities to achieve the defined business objectives.

Data management frameworks such as the Enterprise Data Management (EDM) Council's Data Management Capability Assessment Model (DCAM) and Cloud Data Management Capabilities (CDMC) offer a structured way to assess data maturity against industry benchmarks with a common language and set of data best practices.

The next step is to look at how data is currently being governed and managed within the organization. What are the strengths and weaknesses of current approaches? What is needed to deliver key business objectives?

Organizations don't have to (nor should they) do everything at once. Identify areas for improvement, in the context of business objectives, to prioritize efforts and focus on the most important areas to deliver results to the business in a meaningful way. An effective and efficient data-governance program will support an organization's growth and competitive advantage.

Step 4: Document the organization's data policies.

Data policies are a set of documented guidelines for how an organization's data assets are consistently governed, managed, protected, and used. Data policies are driven by the organization's data strategy, align against business objectives and desired outcomes, and may be influenced by internal and external regulatory factors. Data policies may include topics such as data collection, storage, usage, quality, and security.

Data policies are designed to ensure that data is being used in a way that supports the overall goals of the organization and complies with relevant laws and regulations. This can lead to improved data quality, better decision-making, and increased trust in the organization's data assets, ultimately leading to a more successful and sustainable organization.

Step 5: Establish roles and responsibilities.

Define clear roles and responsibilities of the people involved in data governance, including those responsible for collecting, storing, and using data. This will help ensure everyone understands their role and can effectively contribute to the data-governance effort.

The structure of data governance can vary depending on the organization. In a large enterprise, data governance may have a dedicated team overseeing it, while in a small business, data governance may be part of existing roles and responsibilities. A hybrid approach may also be suitable for some organizations. It's crucial to consider company culture and to develop a data-governance framework that promotes data-driven practices. The key to success is to start small, learn, and adapt, while focusing on delivering and measuring business outcomes.

Having a clear understanding of the roles and responsibilities of data-governance participants can ensure that they have the necessary skills and knowledge to perform their duties.

Step 6: Develop and refine data processes.

Data-governance processes ensure effective decision-making and enable consistent data-management practices by coordinating teams across (and outside of) the organization. Additionally, data-governance processes can ensure compliance with regulatory standards and protect sensitive data.

Data processes provide formal channels for direction, escalation, and resolution. Data-governance processes should be lightweight to achieve the desired business goals without adding unnecessary burdens or hindering innovation. Processes may be automated through tools, workflow, and technology.

It's important to establish these processes early to prevent issues or confusion that may arise later in the data-management implementation.

Step 7: Implement, evaluate, and adapt the strategy.

Having defined the components of the data-governance program, it's time to put them in action. This could include implementing new technologies or processes or making changes to existing ones.

It's important to remember that data-governance programs can be successful only if they demonstrate value to the business, so there's a need to measure and report on the delivery of the prioritized business outcomes. Regularly monitoring and reviewing the strategy will ensure that it's meeting the defined goals and business objectives.

Continually evaluate goals and objectives and adjust as needed. This will enable the data-governance program to evolve and adapt to the changing needs of the organization and the industry. An approach of continual improvement will enable the data-governance program to stay relevant and deliver maximum value to the organization.

Realizing the Business Value

In conclusion, by following an incremental, structured approach and engaging key stakeholders, it's possible to build a data-governance program that aligns with the unique needs of the organization and supports the delivery of accelerated business outcomes.

Implementing a data-governance program can present unique challenges, such as limited resources, resistance to change, and a lack of understanding of the value of data governance. These challenges can be overcome by effectively communicating the value and benefits of the program to all stakeholders, providing training and support to those responsible for implementation, and involving key decision-makers in the planning process.

By implementing a data-governance program that delivers key business outcomes, an organization can ensure the success of the program and drive measurable business value from the organization's data assets while effectively managing data, improving data quality, and maintaining the integrity of data throughout its lifecycle.

Technology Building Blocks of Data Governance

The key technology elements necessary to successfully implementing a data-governance program include the following:

- **Augmented data cataloging:** A data catalog with a rich and metadata-driven index of cataloged assets can help users more easily find and use the right data. It can act as a system of record to capture and manage the portfolio of governed data and analytics assets, policies, and other governance artifacts throughout the data product lifecycle. Using robust search methods, AI recommendations, and user reviews, an intelligent data catalog can provide a strong marketplace experience for well-described and well-governed data assets.

- **Automated metadata generation:** Metadata tracks the origin, privacy level, age, and potential uses of your data. Manually generating metadata is cumbersome, but with ML, data can be automatically tagged with metadata to mitigate human error and dark data. Automatic tagging of the metadata enables policy enforcement at the point of access so that sensitive data can be used in a non-identifiable and compliant way. In addition, metadata is used to link data from different sources and to establish a common vocabulary of business terms that provide context to data. This context adds semantic meaning to data so that it becomes more findable, usable, and consistent within the organization, a key factor when seeking data for analytics and AI.

- **Automated data access and lineage:** Data lineage shows, traces, and analyzes how data is moved and consumed across all of an organization's applications and data sources. Knowing where data comes from is useful not only for compliance reporting, but also for building trustworthy and explainable AI models. Also, it can be automated without complicating access. With restrictions built directly into access points—for example, dynamic data masking—only data that users are authorized to access will be visible. This clarity around what data can and can't be used supports self-service data demands and enables organizations to be nimble in responding to line-of-business needs.

- **Data privacy management:** An open and intelligent approach to accessing, curating, and sharing data across an organization can not only increase compliance with data privacy and industry regulations, but also enhance the ability to make data-driven decisions. First, identify where sensitive data lives across the data estate(s). Next, identify and protect sensitive data from unauthorized users with data policy management, which describes how data should be handled and automated through data protection, data quality, and automation rules. As sensitive data is consumed within key endpoints across a distributed data landscape, data protection rules to anonymize data or deny access can be automatically applied according to user and data attributes.

- **Data quality management:** The quality of data impacts how confidently an organization can act on insights. If low-quality data enters AI models, it could lead to inaccurate, non-compliant, or discriminatory results. Low-quality data also affects operational and analytical use cases. Getting the best insights means being able to access data that is fresh, clean, and relevant and that follows a consistent taxonomy. Organizations must address data-quality issues with critical data elements by assigning data-quality scores to assets and must simplify curation through AI-driven data-quality rules with an automated, metadata-driven foundation. Organizations must also mitigate the potential impact of bad-quality data on downstream processes by using data observability capabilities to monitor and identify data-quality issues closer to the source.

- **Data virtualization:** Data virtualization connects data across all locations and makes the disparate data sources appear as a single database or data source. This helps ensure compliant access to the data through governed data access, regardless of where it lives, without movement. Using the single, virtualized governed layer, user access to data is defined in one place instead of at each source, reducing complexity of access management.

- **Reporting and auditing:** Organizations must comply with a wide variety of changing regulations that differ according to geography, industry, and data type. These regulations need to be broken down into a catalog of requirements with a clear set of actions that businesses must take. Regulatory information should be automatically ingested, deduplicated, and applied to workflows. The secret to harmonizing all these data privacy and governance needs with business opportunity is aligning the technology components with a global data strategy and an open and holistic architecture.

Taking a Data-Fabric Approach to Implementing Data Governance

To harness data for insights and business growth—and ultimately create a data-driven culture—organizations need a holistic approach to data architecture and a strategy that's efficient and doesn't involve manually patching together many solutions. Therefore, many organizations are adopting a data-fabric approach.

A modern data architecture ensures data is accessible to relevant data users based on their unique workflows. Data fabric is an architectural approach that simplifies data access in an organization and facilitates self-service data consumption. Teams can use this architecture to automate data discovery, governance, and consumption through integrated end-to-end data-management capabilities. Whether data engineers, data scientists, or business users are the intended audience, a data fabric delivers the data needed for better decision-making.

A data fabric elevates the value of the organization's data by providing the right data at the right time, regardless of where it resides. A data fabric brings together capabilities like those listed previously as part of a unified architecture, avoiding the cost and complexity of integrating a plethora of point solutions. Instead of a fragmented group of products that have been stitched together, a data fabric offers a single, holistic solution that is built to work seamlessly.

An effective data-governance strategy is dependent on a technology stack designed to gain end-to-end governance, deliver quality data, and ultimately accelerate collaboration. The value of data governance is amplified when this capability is combined with data integration and entity-resolution capabilities.

(Entity resolution is the process of determining whether multiple records are referencing the same real-world thing or object.)

As part of a modern data fabric, data governance creates an end-to-end user experience rooted in metadata and active policy management that empowers users to view, access, manipulate, and analyze data without the need to understand its physical format or location and without having to move or copy it. In addition, a data fabric can address three separate use cases beyond data governance and privacy. These use cases are data integration, data science and machine-learning operations (MLOps), and AI governance.

The technology components of the IBM data fabric approach enable companies to automatically apply industry-specific regulatory policies and rules to their data assets, securing them across the enterprise with:

- An AI-augmented data catalog that helps business users easily understand, collaborate on, enrich, and access the right data

- A metadata and governance layer for all data, analytics, and AI initiatives that increases visibility and collaboration on any cloud

- The ability to mask data dynamically and consistently at a user-defined granular level

- The ability to create anonymized training data and test sets while maintaining data integrity

AI Governance

AI has progressed to become an integral part of enterprise strategy at companies large and small. It presents an enormous opportunity to turn data into insights, spark action that's based on better decision-making, and amplify human capabilities for the greater good—and for better business. AI can help decrease business risk and increase ROI by making breakthrough innovations possible. However, the promise of AI isn't guaranteed. Responsible, transparent, and explainable AI doesn't come easy.

Taking a Responsible Approach to AI

As the outcomes of AI models and insights become more business-critical, models need to operate reliably with visibility and accountability during processes. Analytic decisions based on incomplete or inaccurate data, models, workflows, or processes can have dire consequences. Success requires automation and transparency across the AI lifecycle, coupled with documented, explainable results.

Leaders of enterprises creating AI services are being challenged by an emerging problem of how to effectively govern the creation, deployment, and management of these services throughout the AI lifecycle. Today's enterprises, including IBM, want to understand and have control over their processes to meet internal policies and external regulations.

This is where AI governance makes a difference. AI governance is the overall process of directing, managing, and monitoring the AI activities of an organization. Whether an organization is considering adopting AI or is further along the journey, establishing an AI governance framework should be part of the strategy. Organizations that stay proactive and infuse governance into their AI initiatives from the onset can help minimize risk while strengthening their ability to meet ethical principles and comply with government regulations. Leaders of organizations and enterprises in regulated industries, such as banking and financial services, are legally required to provide a certain level of transparency in their AI models to satisfy regulators.

The Challenges of Scaling AI

The influence of AI is growing exponentially as organizations deploy it in banking, transportation, healthcare, education, farming, retail, and many other industries. At the same time, employees and leaders at many of these organizations have difficulty with the following aspects of implementing AI:

- **Operationalizing AI with confidence:** There's a wide variety of tools for AI governance, but too often models are built without proper clarity, monitoring, or cataloging. That includes a lack of tracking through the end-to-end AI lifecycle, a lack of automated processes for scale, and a lack of transparency and explainability. Readers may have heard of "black box models," which are a growing concern for AI stakeholders. Black box AI models are built and deployed, but it isn't always easy to trace how and why decisions were made, even for the data scientists who created them. These challenges lead to inefficiencies resulting in scope drift, models that are delayed or never placed into production, or models that have inconsistent levels of quality and unperceived risks.

- **Managing risk and reputation:** Readers may have seen the stories in the press complaining of unfair, unexplainable, or biased models in production. These issues can result in incorrect assumptions and decisions, which affect customers and can harm an organization's brand. Explainable processes and results are crucial if a compliance auditor or customer wants to know how specific analytic results were reached and are key to ensuring that results don't reflect bias around race, gender, age, or other common factors. Scenarios in which explainability is critical include patient medical diagnoses and treatment plans, transactions flagged as suspicious, and loan applications that are denied. That's why it's important to practice responsible AI. Responsible AI is an approach that results in AI systems that are transparent, explainable, fair, and inclusive—preserving privacy, security, customer loyalty, and trust.

- **Responding to changing AI regulations:** Successful and responsible AI requires an awareness of local, regional, national, and international laws and regulations, which are growing at a rapid pace. Noncompliance may ultimately cost an organization millions of dollars in fines, as demonstrated by some of the most stringent AI regulations being debated around the world, like the proposed EU AI Act. The current draft of the EU AI Act contemplates fines of up to €30 million or 6 percent of a company's global revenue, whichever is higher for infringements and even higher for non-compliance. Model documentation is key for regulatory compliance—an area with aspects easy to miss for a data scientist pressed for time and whose organization lacks clear requirements. Because new regulations will require model documentation for metadata and lineage, this step is especially important. Figure 5.2 shows a timeline of some of the key global AI regulations.

Timeline of global AI regulation

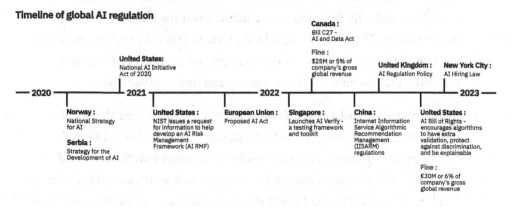

Figure 5.2: Timeline of some of the key global AI regulations

The Building Blocks of AI Governance

Like any other initiative, successful AI governance depends upon the intersection of people, process, and technology.

- **People and objectives**: To implement AI properly, organizations need a strong cross-functional team. AI continues to be a strategic imperative for many leaders, and it can feel like the list of stakeholders grows longer by the day. Some of these people are new to the AI lifecycle concept, while others have new reasons to be involved in AI efforts. Organizations must try to meet the needs of each of these groups without overburdening data scientists, who often have little time to route or manage the approvals and requests for information.

  Start by putting stakeholders into alignment. Get buy-in from the right interested parties and encourage them to participate in ideation, align on outcomes, and adopt responsible AI. Then, take steps to ensure that the correct set of metrics, KPIs, and objectives are defined in accordance with an organization's business controls and regulations. Organizations will need to monitor the specific metrics that have been identified for their AI models. Figure 5.3 shows some of the key roles across the AI lifecycle.

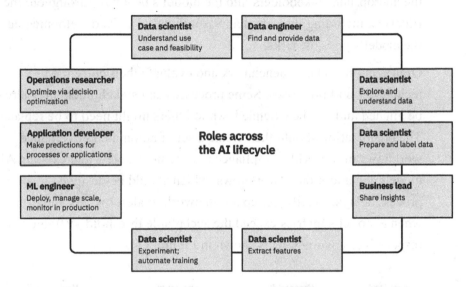

Figure 5.3: Roles across the AI lifecycle

Encourage collaboration with key stakeholders and understand their top concerns:

- CFO, risks to profitability

- CMO, risks to brand

- CRO, risks to enterprise

- CDO, efficient data operations

- CHRO, potential talent impacts

- CEO, organizational accountability

- CPO, regulatory accountability

- **Process:** AI governance traces and documents for audit purposes the origin of data, associated models and metadata, and overall data pipelines. Documentation should include the techniques that trained each model, the hyperparameters that were used, and the metrics from testing phases. This results in increased transparency and visibility by the appropriate stakeholders into the model's behavior throughout the lifecycle, including the data that was influential in its development and the model's possible risks.

Organizations need to benchmark and evaluate their current AI technology and processes. Some processes and stakeholders may already be aligned and can be extended, while others might need to be replaced. The organization should then create a set of automated governance workflows in line with compliance requirements. New and existing AI models can adopt these workflows, which should be designed to avoid process delays. Finally, set up a framework to alert owners and users when a model's metrics exceed the acceptable threshold. A framework for responsible, governed AI is shown in Figure 5.4.

	Operationalize with confidence	Manage risk and reputation	Strengthen compliance	Meet stakeholder demands
Plan	Define measurable performance metrics for AI usage across your organization	Review existing processes that monitor fairness and explainability	Conduct gap analysis against current and potential AI regulations	Review existing skills and demand for responsible AI, and align with business objectives
Build	Establish traceability and audit ability of current processes	Operationalize updated processes and checkpoints throughout the AI lifecycle	Make sure model documentation is accessible	Specify the new roles, skills, and learning agendas required to implement responsible AI
Create	Create automatic documentation of model lineage and metadata	Enable high-quality AI models that are fair and explainable that minimize drift and conduct regular policy reviews	Act to strengthen regulatory compliance for data science teams without adding overhead	Establish a repeatable end-to-end workflow with built-in stakeholder approvals to lower risk and increase scale

Figure 5.4: A framework for responsible, governed AI

- **Technology:** The establishment of well-planned, well-executed, and well-controlled AI requires specific technological building blocks. Look for a solution that governs the end-to-end AI lifecycle and has the following capabilities:

  - Integrates data of many types and sources across diverse deployments

  - Is open and flexible and works with an organization's existing tools of choice

  - Offers self-service access with privacy controls and a way to track lineage

  - Automates model building, deployment, scaling, training, and monitoring

  - Connects multiple stakeholders through a customizable workflow

  - Provides support to build customized workflows for different personas using governance metadata

The watsonx.governance Solution

The IBM approach to AI governance is designed to help organizations direct, manage, and monitor an organization's AI activities. Built on the IBM Cloud Pak for Data platform, this governance solution employs software automation to strengthen the ability to meet regulatory requirements and address ethical concerns. Organizations expect a comprehensive AI governance solution without the excessive costs of switching from current data-science platforms. This solution spans the entire lifecycle, including designing, building, deploying, monitoring, and centralizing facts for AI explainability, as shown in Figure 5.5.

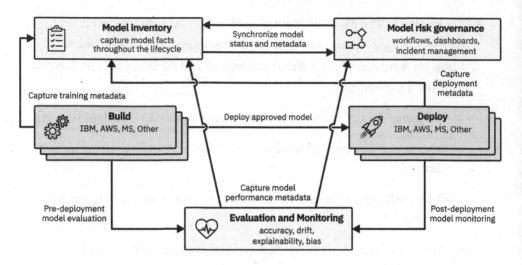

Figure 5.5: watsonx.governance integrates with existing ML development and deployment

Before a model is put into production, it's validated to assess the risks to the business. Once the model goes live, it's continuously monitored for fairness, quality, and drift. Regulators and auditors can be provided with access to the model's documentation, which provides explanations of the model's behavior and predictions. These explanations provide visibility into how the model works and what processes and training the model received.

With this solution, audits can become easier. An organization will be able to trace and document the origin of data, the models and associated metadata, and the pipelines. The documentation will include the techniques that trained each model, the hyperparameters used, and the metrics from testing phases. Organizations can benefit from having increased transparency into the model's behavior throughout the lifecycle, knowledge of the data that was influential in its development, and the ability to determine possible risks. Figure 5.6 shows some of the key governance components organizations need to consider.

Lifecycle governance

- Monitor, catalog, and govern AI models from where they reside
- Automate the capture of model metadata
- Increase prediction accuracy, identifying how AI is used and where it lags

Comprehensive

Govern the end-to-end AI lifecycle.

Risk management

- Automate facts and workflow for compliance to business standards
- Identify, manage, monitor, and report on risk and compliance, at scale
- Use dynamic dashboards for clear, concise, customizable results
- Enhance collaboration across multiple regions and geographies

Open

Support governance of models built and deployed in third-party tools.

Regulatory compliance

- Translate external AI regulations into policies for automated enforcement
- Enhance adherence to regulations for audit and compliance
- Use dynamic dashboards for compliance across policies and regulations

Automatic metadata

Data transformation and lineage capture through Python notebooks.

Figure 5.6: Key governance components to consider

Benefits of Governance Using a Lakehouse

Governance is far-reaching, almost ubiquitous. Every asset created, used, tested, deployed, and managed is subject to governance across many personas (enterprise user roles). A lakehouse, combining data and technologies from both enterprise data warehouses and data lakes, drives the need for a more diverse and complete set of governance capabilities essential to a successful implementation. While understanding the capabilities provided by watsonx. governance (discussed above), governance is also deeply ingrained into the data fabric, as shown in Figure 5.7. It's also part of the governance and metadata layer within watsonx.data, providing the three levels of access controls mentioned in an earlier chapter:

- **User Authentication (Level 1 access control):** watsonx.data works with a variety of Identity Provider Services, such as Identity Access Management (IAM) or Lightweight Directory Access Protocol (LDAP). Users who access the service through UIs, APIs, SQL editors, and command lines will be authenticated using their user ID and password, API keys, or authentication tokens.

- **User Access to Resources (Level 2 access control):** Roles can be assigned for watsonx.data users to access lakehouse resources. Roles at this level include Viewer, Editor, and Administrator. Resources include instances, engines, catalogs, storage, and databases.

- **User Access to Data (Level 3 access control):** watsonx.data enables data administrators to define data access policies for deeper levels of governance. Access policies can be defined on schemas, tables, columns, and rows. Users are checked for access based on defined access policies. Advanced governance involving the masking of data, for example, leverages IBM Knowledge Catalog governance.

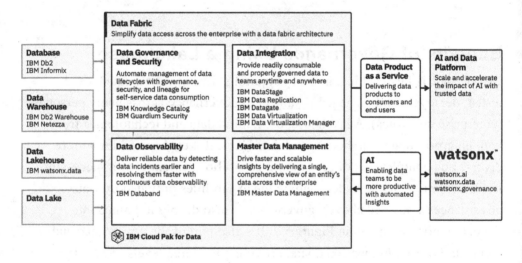

Figure 5.7: Data-fabric governance: delivering Data Product as a Service to watsonx.data and the wider watsonx platform

The combined governance capabilities across watsonx.governance, watsonx.data, the data-fabric services within Cloud Pak for Data, and services within other Cloud Paks ensure data governance, AI governance, and security is engrained and embedded into all elements of the IBM watsonx platform.

Furthermore, such embedding of governance capabilities helps unlock several capabilities, such as tracking data lineage, building a deep understanding of the data in the lakehouse via classification and association of business terms, masking sensitive data based on policies, and ensuring data privacy and security. For example, these data governance capabilities enable clients to profile the data in the lakehouse to identify data classes such as Personal Identifiable Information (PII), Sensitive Personal Information (SPI), credit card numbers, etc. Such classification also helps associate the right business terms to the data in the lakehouse. These business terms can be further used to enforce policies, such as tables containing credit card numbers that should be masked before they are shared with third-party vendors. Thus, data governance plays a crucial role in ensuring that the data in the lakehouse is understood, profiled, classified, and accessed in a safe and secure manner.

Data lakehouse implementations such as watsonx.data also play a critical role in satisfying the AI governance needs of enterprises. As an example, financial services sector (FSS) clients have a set of standard best practices that mandate what happens after a data science team has built an AI model that is handed over to the model validation team—also referred to as the model risk management (MRM) team. As per best practices, MRM teams try to recreate the AI model by following the same set of steps that the data scientist employed. This includes using the same training data, framework, algorithm, and hyperparameters used to train the model. Such a procedure is adopted to ensure that the MRM team can recreate the model from scratch, evaluate the quality of the model, and ensure that it is in line with the quality reported by the data scientists. This ensures that there is proper cross-validation of the technique and the results obtained by the data scientists before an AI model is deployed to production.

IBM's AI governance capabilities help the MRM team to understand the training data, framework, algorithm, parameters, and other factors that were used by the data scientists to build the model (because all of this is captured as governance metadata). However, the MRM team is often unable to achieve the same results as those obtained by the data scientists. The reason for this is that there is a delay between the data scientists building the model and it being evaluated by the MRM team, sometimes more than a month. This means the data scientists could have built the model using the training data from a table as it existed when they built the AI model. That table would have been updated over the intervening period, and when the MRM team tried to recreate the model, the team made use of the updated data in the table, thereby getting a different model, which leads to different model-quality results.

This problem can be easily solved if the training data is stored in the lakehouse. A lakehouse such as watsonx.data provides the capability of "time travel," which enables the MRM team to recreate a snapshot of the table as it existed when the data scientists built the model. This solves what was a challenging problem because the MRM teams can build the exact same model and deliver the same model-quality results as were obtained by the data scientists when the model was first built. This helps the MRM team cross-check the results of the data scientists and ensure proper validation of the model before it's deployed to production.

The time travel capability to recreate the training data is also useful when clients need to prove to the regulators that the AI models they are using were fair and of high quality when they were built by their data science teams.

Governance Success Story

A bank sought to address revenue loss due to attrition among their private-wealth clients. The bank was hindered by the reliance on siloed data sets, development teams working in isolation, and inconsistent development methods. This led to inconsistent business results and doubts about whether a generated AI solution met ethical standards.

Working with IBM, the bank was able to transform how it generated the AI solution by using modern tools, processes, and new open, transparent methodologies. The bank adopted enhanced ML pipelines for private-wealth-retention models to better detect drift in model accuracy and data consistency in their production data lake. The solution adopted used IBM Expert Labs, IBM AI Governance, and IBM Watson Studio.

The results have been trusted analytic solutions that help reduce risk, detect fraud, assist commercial customers, and provide insights into customers' needs. The benefits to the bank include the ability to:

- Standardize monitoring of models in the end-to-end ML pipelines.

- Provide a continuous read on accuracy of predictions in production.

- Automate model retraining based on monitoring alerts.

- Identify wealth clients with low-confidence predictions.

Scaling Automation to Address AI Regulatory Requirements

Building on IBM's AI framework to address AI regulatory requirements, IBM's Chief Privacy Officer (CPO) has taken significant steps in putting into practice AI and data industry-leading capabilities built on a strong combination of privacy, security, AI governance, ethics, processes, technology, and tooling.

The IBM CPO, supported by the IBM AI Ethics Board, developed a set of enhanced processes that enable more detailed tracking of compliance with existing standards and applicable legal requirements. Using IBM's integrated governance framework and processes to manage and monitor the development and use of AI across the company, teams can:

- Create a robust workflow using IBM tools to collect, consolidate, display, and monitor the workflow.

- Automate the capture and integration of facts from the AI lifecycle to accelerate the maintenance of the global AI inventory.

AI Ethics

In a world where trust, transparency, and explainable AI matter, every organizational leader wants a better understanding of how analytic insights and decisions are being made—and every leader is serious about regulatory compliance. The purpose of AI is to augment human intelligence, affirm that data and insights belong to their creator, and ensure that new technology—including AI systems—is transparent and explainable.

Today, AI permeates every aspect of business function. Whether it be financial services, employee hiring, customer service management, or healthcare administration, AI is increasingly powering critical workflows across all industries. However, with greater AI adoption comes greater challenges. In the marketplace, we have seen numerous missteps involving inaccurate outcomes, unfair recommendations, and other unwanted consequences. This has created concerns among both private and public organizations as to whether AI is being used responsibly. Add navigating complex compliance regulations and standards to the mix, and the need for a solid and trustworthy AI strategy becomes clear.

To scale use of AI in a responsible manner requires AI governance, the process of defining policies and establishing accountability throughout the AI lifecycle. This in turn requires an AI ethics policy, as only by embedding ethical principles into AI applications and processes can we build systems based on trust.

IBM Research has been developing trustworthy AI tools since 2012. When IBM launched its AI Ethics Board (see https://www.ibm.com/impact/ai-ethics) in 2018, AI ethics was not a hot topic in the press, nor was it top of mind among business leaders. However, as AI has become essential, touching on so many aspects of daily life, the interest in AI ethics has grown exponentially.

In a 2021 study by the IBM Institute for Business Value (available at www.ibm.com/downloads/cas/4DPJK92W), nearly 75 percent of executives ranked AI ethics as important, a jump from less than 50 percent in 2018. What's more, suggests the study, those organizations that implement a broad AI ethics strategy, interwoven throughout business units, may have a competitive advantage moving forward.

The Principles of AI Ethics

At IBM, we believe building trustworthy AI requires a multidisciplinary, multidimensional approach based on the following three ethical principles (see https://www.ibm.com/impact/ai-ethics):

- **The purpose of AI is to augment human intelligence, not replace it.** At IBM, we believe AI should be designed and built to enhance and extend human capability and potential.

- **Data and insights belong to their creator.** IBM clients' data is their data, and their insights are their insights. We believe that data policies should be fair and equitable and prioritize openness.

- **Technology must be transparent and explainable.** Companies must be clear about who trains their AI systems, what data was used in training, and, most importantly, what went into their algorithms' recommendations.

When thinking about what it takes to really earn trust in decisions made by AI, leaders should ask themselves five human-centric questions: Is it easy to understand? Is it fair? Did anyone tamper with it? Is it accountable? Does it safeguard data? These questions translate into five fundamental principles for trustworthy AI: fairness, robustness, privacy, explainability, and transparency (see https://www.ibm.com/policy/ibm-artificial-intelligence-pillars/).

When discussing AI governance, it's important to be conscious of two distinct aspects coming together:

- **Organizational AI governance** encompasses deciding and driving AI strategy for an organization. This includes establishing AI policies for the organization based on AI principles, regulations, and laws.

- **AI model governance** introduces technology to implement guardrails at each stage of the AI/ML lifecycle. This includes data collecting, process instrumentation, and transparent reporting to make needed information available for all the stakeholders.

Often, organizations looking for trustworthy solutions in the form of AI governance require guidance on one or both fronts.

Scaling Trustworthy AI

Recently, an American multinational financial institution came to IBM with several challenges, including deploying ML models in the hundreds that were built using multiple stacks of open-source and third-party tools. The Chief Data Officer (CDO) saw that it was essential for the company to have a holistic framework that would work with the models built across the company using diverse tools.

In this case, IBM Expert Labs collaborated with the financial institution to create a technology-led solution using IBM Cloud Pak for Data. The result was an AI governance hub built at enterprise scale, which enables the CDO to track and govern hundreds of AI models for compliance across the bank, irrespective of the ML tools used.

Sometimes an organization's need is more tied to organizational AI governance. For instance, a multinational healthcare organization wanted to expand an AI model that was being used to infer technical skills to now infer soft/foundational skills. The company brought in members of IBM Consulting to train the organization's team of data scientists on how to use frameworks for systemic empathy, well before code was written, to consider intent and safeguard rails for models. After the success of this session, the client saw the need for broader AI governance. With help from IBM Consulting, the company established its first AI ethics board, a center of excellence, and an AI literacy program.

In many instances, enterprise-level organizations need a hybrid approach to AI governance. Recently, a French banking group was faced with new compliance measures. The company did not have enough organizational processes and automated AI model monitoring in place to address AI governance at scale. The team also wanted to establish a culture to responsibly curate AI. They needed both organizational AI governance and AI model-governance solutions.

IBM Consulting worked with the client to establish a set of AI principles and an ethics board to address the many upcoming regulations. This effort, working together with IBM Expert Labs services, implemented the technical solution components, such as an enterprise AI workflow, monitors for bias, performance, and drift, and generated fact sheets for the AI models to promote transparency across the broader organization.

Establishing both organizational and AI model governance to operationalize AI ethics requires a holistic approach. IBM offers services and capabilities for an organization's AI governance journey:

- IBM Expert Labs for a technology solution that provides guardrails across all stages of the AI lifecycle

- IBM Consulting for a holistic approach to socio-technological challenges

6

REAL-WORLD, INDUSTRY-SPECIFIC USE CASES

IBM Cloud Pak technologies form a strong foundation on which watsonx leverages many AI, data, automation, and security services. Cloud Pak for Data, for example, embeds a set of unified, integrated data and AI services and capabilities for delivering and supporting a data fabric. Based on numerous IBM engagements and thousands of deployments worldwide, we highlight a number of use cases involving Cloud Pak for Data and watsonx.data across multiple industries drawn from more than 140 external references. These have been anonymized to protect the identity of the account names.

Banking and Financial Markets

Business Challenge

A financial services company servicing student loans in the US expected a considerable uptick of customer questions because of COVID-19. The client anticipated a huge spike of requests for alternate repayment options. With more than 4 million website visits per month, the client wanted to set up a Watson virtual assistant for its customers. Pressured for time, the company needed to deploy a solution within a matter of weeks.

Solution

IBM Cloud Pak for Data was the answer to the problem. IBM's platform enabled the company to continue using their own compliant version of Microsoft Azure and still leverage IBM watsonx Assistant. Because the company is involved with student loans, it needed a robust solution that could get approval from the federal Department of Education. Part of that requirement included being able to run within a Federal Information Processing Standards (FIPS)-enabled solution data center, which meant the center had to meet federally mandated security protocols. Cloud Pak for Data gave the client that flexibility and opened a virtual assistant as a top option for their customers to receive secure support.

Outcome

- A complete working solution that is FIPS-enabled and approved by the Department of Education was delivered in seven weeks.

- IBM watsonx Assistant has 90 million monthly active users servicing 3,000 clients.

Healthcare

Business Challenge

There is a big challenge in preventing secondary injuries for traumatic brain injury (TBI) patients. Intracranial hypertension crises, a major reason for secondary injuries, are often identified late and managed reactively. Neurosurgeons are currently looking at a variety of physiological time-series data to make treatment decisions, but monitoring for intracranial pressure (ICP) crises is a manual and labor-intensive process. Neurointensivists are looking for ways to be more proactive in their treatment of ICP crisis events, which they believe will lead to better patient outcomes.

Solution

IBM's Data Science and AI Elite team developed an ML model that can predict increases in ICP with a lead time of 20–30 minutes, providing enough time for neurosurgeons to intervene and potentially avoid crises. The data-driven solution leveraged ML by uncovering hidden patterns within the physiological time-series data. The model could provide continuous prediction at regular intervals and, if implemented in clinical workflows, could potentially improve patient outcomes after severe TBI.

Outcome

- IBM created an ML model to predict ICP crises as a binary outcome with a lead time of 20–30 minutes.

- The solution reduces the manual and labor-intensive process of monitoring for ICP to detect increases in ICP.

- The solution has the potential to improve patient outcomes after TBI if implemented in clinical workflows.

Government and Federal

Business Challenge

Recurrent homelessness has become a significant cost driver for a Department of Social Services in North America and a problem that contributes to chronic homelessness. The goal was for the department to become equipped and trained with the appropriate AI tools to predict and understand the factors that lead someone back to homelessness and identify actions the department could take to help those people.

Solution

IBM Data Science and AI Elite team collaborated with the Department of Social Services to co-create a proof-of-concept solution to use IBM's Cloud Pak for Data to bring together data from various sources and develop an ML model that predicted whether an individual would be at risk of recurrence in the next six months. With the ability to produce accurate predictions and explanations, the department expects to proactively mitigate homelessness by gaining insights into the factors that contribute to local homeless recurrence.

Outcome

- The final model achieved 92 percent accuracy in predicting the probability of an individual re-entering a shelter within the next six months.

- The model increased transparency in data analysis and model predictions.

Retail and Consumer Products

Business Challenge

In retail cybercrime, there is significant data and revenue loss as well as security and privacy concerns that are sensitive to each retailer. Due to differences in data collection and organization among the retailers, cross-retailer data analysis and collaboration is challenging, decentralized, and inaccurate. Because of this, verifying the same perpetrators across different retailers has proved almost impossible, preventing the opportunity to build a single case for prosecution against such individuals.

Solution

With IBM's Data Science Elite team using Watson Studio and Cloud Pak for Data, a constructed model was able to extract name and license plate data-matching from retailer databases, which provided an initial pass at providing cross-retailer cases for the same individuals or groups. Fuzzy matching (FM) provided additional perpetrator crime matches using a spectrum of similarity thresholds. Using Doc2Vec to create vector representations of incident narratives enabled use of automated assessments of similarities between free-text descriptions of similar crimes. These three methodologies were implemented to find individuals or groups committed to organized crime across eight major retailers. This operation was then handed over to IBM Cloud Garage for further development and extension.

Outcome

- The solution provided identification and verification of common perpetrators across eight major retailers.

- The solution offered metadata collection, including monetary value of crimes, number of crimes, and number of retailers targeted for prioritization.

- The solution was the first automated attempt to fight retail organized crime, currently valued at a $2.1 billion loss across the US.

Technology

Business Challenge

With increasingly complex regulatory requirements and the necessity for self-service, the centralized data lake residing in IBM's Global Chief Data Office (GCDO) was becoming insufficient and infeasible. IBM's GCDO focuses on delivering trusted, enterprise-wide data and services to IBM. IBM has experienced the many challenges of this mission firsthand, and in response it has embraced an enterprise-wide data-fabric strategy.

Solution

IBM's GCDO embraced the vision of data fabric and leveraged Cloud Pak for Data heavily. Several pieces of the data-fabric solution have been developed and are in production. Key capabilities that have been developed and deployed include abilities to collect, catalog, analyze, and understand enterprise data where it resides and to take measures of data-related KPIs (including quality, compliance with enterprise data standards, and methods by which data flows between systems). IBM Knowledge Catalog enables users to self-serve data with appropriate access privileges, across a hybrid multi-cloud data architecture with efficient and trusted data movement. Streamlining the data pipelines using DataOps principles to provide quality data with lineage tracking provided better insight generation. Data Discovery and semantic search using ontologies enabled knowledge workers to find data using intuitive business language.

Outcome

- Data fabric enables data integration across heterogenous and distributed data landscapes at scale.

- GCDO was asked by a sales team to develop a program supporting 50 opportunities worth more than $5 million. Leveraging data fabric and the MD360 solution supported this request, saving many hours for marketing staff and sellers and decreasing overall cycle time.

Telecommunications

Business Challenge

A large telecommunications company operates cell towers around the clock and was looking for an opportunity to reduce power costs and CO_2 emissions by intentionally switching off cell layers for specific durations with minimal customer impact. The key challenge was to identify the sweet spot between cost-savings and an unacceptable impact to customer experience.

Solution

A constructed model sifted through a large variety of data sources across all the cell layers and inferred users' activities and the power costs associated with them. With the inputs from a segmentation model, a forecasting model, customer impact costs, and other business constraints, the decision optimization capability was able to generate a power-saving schedule that reduced cell-tower operating hours while minimizing the impact to customer experience.

Outcome

- The solution resulted in a 41 percent reduction in operating hours of cell layers with a 5 percent customer impact.

- The solution produced a $90,000 projected savings per year for 215 cell sites.

- The solution produced a 93 percent network-traffic load-forecasting accuracy.

- The solution enabled a 99 percent power-saving reduction.

Energy and Utilities

Business Challenge

A large energy company wanted to reinvent itself as a data-driven organization in which data science capabilities were readily accessible across multiple business units. The client struggled with siloed data, inconsistent tools, and various skill levels, causing critical explainability difficulties.

Solution

In 2018, the IBM Data Science and AI Elite team engaged with the client's analytics group to set a strategy for an integrated data and AI platform that could be used as a centralized solution for multiple business units. IBM Cloud Pak for Data plus IBM Watson Machine Learning Accelerator was chosen as that platform and was installed for initial use in March 2019.

The following use cases have been implemented on Cloud Pak for Data:

- eMobility
- COVID-19 load impacts
- Return-to-work risk model
- Gas operations document discovery and handwriting extraction
- Electric customer segmentation and load forecasting
- Asset management
- Market research
- Web marketing

Outcome

- Multiple business units now have access to a self-service data and AI platform.
- The client has the ability to use fit-for-purpose compute capacity to run models on billions of rows of data records.
- The client can collaboratively develop and deploy the models to infuse insight throughout the company.

Distribution

Business Challenge

A North American retail corporation manages replenishment orders for five countries for 36,000 products from 3,800 vendors. In a typical 30-day cycle, a team of experienced planners perform the complex task of determining the exact amounts of products to order from each vendor, such that containers remain optimally filled, reducing long-term shipping costs as well as excess inventory while meeting customer demand.

Solution

IBM's Data Science and AI Elite team built a proof of concept (POC) IBM Decision Optimization CPLEX model to generate weekly vendor-order quantities. The model runs within a few minutes, saving about 90–99 percent of manual processing time, which has the potential to reduce the review time to seven days, enabling an equivalent reduction in inventory. The solution showed the corporation's Central America team how to better build their data pipeline and improve their data QA process. This solution has the potential to reduce 84 percent of long-term cost previously lost from manual processing, better optimize the company's human resources, and improve service by having better capacity to plan with the commercial team.

Outcome

- The solution produced an 84 percent potential for long-term cost reduction: processing, shipping, and inventory costs.

- The solution enabled a 77 percent potential reduction in order-review time, from 30 days to seven days.

- The solution produced a 90-99 percent reduction in manual processing time, from three hours to a few minutes.

Industrial Product

Business Challenge

IBM was introduced to a client's supply-chain department through the Association for Supply Chain Management (ASCM), which wanted to define a joint business case around supply-chain efforts. The goal was to show how data science, ML, decision optimization, and AI could reduce the client's supply-chain risks and the number of model scenarios and fluctuations, as well as minimize inventory and transportation costs.

Solution

To avoid disruptions in the future, the IBM Data Science and AI Elite team challenged foundational systems and processes at the client for one of their largest drug products. The solution was to provide insights into performance of the supply chain to take immediate action based on prescriptive models and stress-test modeling for greater visibility. IBM proposed a platform that can dynamically explore data to find best-fit scenarios and solutions. The platform provides ready access to data at its source without moving it, eliminates data silos, and connects all data to facilitate business decisions.

Outcome

- The solution produced $1.6 million in inventory-reduction savings.

- The solution enabled a 30 percent fee reduction for air-shipping volume.

- The solution produced a 10–15 percent reduction in maintenance, repair, and operations expenses over a three-year period.

Computer Services

Business Challenge

A Czech-based software company, along with an IBM Business Partner, has a mission to deliver innovative AI-based analytical products and elite professional services that help identify potential safety threats in the world. The firm's core customer base spans the public and private sectors: from law enforcement agencies and national intelligence agencies to commercial banks, telco operators, and so much more. These organizations typically have huge amounts of data stored in different formats and locations. Their analytics platform needed a way to collect all these different types of data from customers and link them directly into the firm's platform while also meeting security requirements. The team believed this could greatly speed up the time it takes to process customer data and, more importantly, shorten the amount of time it takes to implement the product with each new customer.

Solution

Building on its longstanding collaboration with IBM, the company partnered with the IBM Client Engineering and Technical Sales teams from the Czech Republic to integrate its solution with IBM watsonx.data. The firm's platform is a secure and user-friendly data analytics solution for investigation, deep dive analysis, pattern searching, and more. The integrated solution is designed to help users collect various types of data—for example, NOSQL, JSON, CSV formatted data—safely and easily using watsonx.data and then connect the data to the company's platform. Users visualize connections and examine the activities of individuals who are involved in an investigation. The platform is designed to make it easier for users to surface insights that support their investigations.

Outcome

The company observed the following results over a 75-day time period:

- Decrease in implementation time by 45 percent for eight tested solutions

- Data from various sources and formats processed up to 60 percent faster.

- Instant automatic linkage with regular data updates from structured and unstructured data sources

Government

Business Challenge

A US law enforcement agency was trying to analyze rapidly growing volumes of data spread across disparate sources to assist officers in searching for and discovering relevant information related to a given case. Investigators were having to spend hours manually sifting through multiple data sources and needed a better way to analyze crime trends.

Solution

Using watsonx.data technology, the agency is able to empower its officers with the information they need for quicker, better planning and decision-making, while spending less time researching and more time serving the public by having rapid access to relevant data in the course of their day-to-day work.

Outcome

- Bringing their existing data sources together

- Spending less time on paperwork

- Allocating more time to solving crimes and serving the community

- Streamlining and consolidating internal reporting, enabling leadership to better analyze weekly crime trends

Aeronautics

Business Challenge

An aeronautics organization involved in advanced scientific discovery, with hundreds of facilities around the globe, is using AI to help its team members discover simple answers to complex questions. In one use case, they needed a way for employees to ask questions about devices and contracted mission times and receive answers in natural language.

Solution

Using IBM watsonx.data, IBM Watson Discovery, and IBM watsonx Assistant solutions, the organization has enabled its employees to use natural language to ask any relevant questions about source data and receive an answer in natural language, without having to do any special coding to handle specific questions.

Outcome

- Increase from 45.45 percent to 56.8 percent of sample questions answered correctly with prompt engineering

- 66.0 percent of questions answered correctly with query optimization

Media and Entertainment

Business Challenge

A major sporting event wanted to enhance the viewer/user experience for its fan base by introducing AI commentary to its tournament as well as introducing hole-by-hole player predictions.

Solution

Leveraging watsonx, multiple foundation models, and IBM Watson Text-to-Speech to train the AI in the unique language of the sport, the team were able to automate the process of adding spoken commentary to video clips. Generative AI built on foundation models was applied to produce narration with varied sentence structure and vocabulary, avoiding redundant play-by-play iterations to make the clips informative and engaging.

Outcome

- Produced detailed sport narration for more than 20,000 video clips over the course of the tournament.

- Expanded on the predictive intelligence of the popular Players Insights and Fantasy Projections feature.

- Turned data into insights around the most exciting parts of the event to watch for every player, showed the low/high score for all players, and projected Fantasy points for every round.

Other Use Cases

These use cases represent a small percentage of organizations and solutions. More use cases can be found at ibm.com/case-studies/search.

7

BUSINESS INTELLIGENCE AND LAKEHOUSES

A Brief History of Business Analytics

The term "business intelligence" (BI) was first used in 1865 by author Richard Millar Devens when he cited a banker who collected intelligence about the market ahead of his competitors. In 1958, an IBM computer scientist named Hans Peter Luhn explored the potential of using technology to gather BI. His research helped establish methods for creating some of IBM's early analytics platforms. In the 1960s and '70s, the first data management systems and decision support systems (DSSs) were developed to store and organize growing volumes of data.

Many historians suggest the modern version of BI evolved from the DSS database. An assortment of tools was developed during that time, with the goal of accessing and organizing data in simpler ways. OLAP, executive information systems, and data warehouses were some of the tools developed to work with DSSs.

By the 1990s, BI grew increasingly popular, but the technology was still complex. It usually required IT support, which often led to backlogs and delayed reports. Even without IT, BI analysts needed extensive training to be able to successfully query and analyze their data.

More-recent development has focused on self-service BI applications, which enable non-expert users to benefit from their own reporting and analysis. Modern cloud-based platforms have also extended the reach of BI across geographies. Many solutions now handle big data and include real-time processing, enabling decision-making processes based on up-to-date information.

Defining Business Intelligence

In essence, BI apps are software that ingests business data and presents it in user-friendly views, such as reports, dashboards, charts, and graphs. BI tools enable business users to access different types of data: historical and current, third-party and in-house, as well as semi-structured data and unstructured data such as social media. Users can analyze this information to gain insights into how a business is performing.

Although BI doesn't tell business users what to do or what will happen if they take a certain course, neither is BI only about generating reports. Rather, BI offers a way for people to examine data to understand trends and derive insights. Organizations can use the insights gained from BI and data analysis to improve business decisions, identify problems or issues, spot market trends, and find new revenue or business opportunities.

BI platforms traditionally rely on data warehouses for their baseline information. A data warehouse aggregates data from multiple data sources into one central system to support business analytics and reporting. BI software queries the warehouse and presents the results to the user in the form of reports, charts, and maps.

Data warehouses can include an online analytical processing (OLAP) engine to support multidimensional queries. For example: What are sales for our eastern region versus our western region this year compared to last year? OLAP provides powerful technology for data discovery, facilitation of BI, complex analytic calculations, and predictive analytics. One of the main benefits of OLAP is the consistency of the information and calculations it uses to drive data to improve product quality, customer interactions, and process enhancements. Some newer BI solutions can extract and ingest raw data directly using technology such as Hadoop, but warehouses have traditionally been the primary data source of choice in most cases.

Benefits of Business Intelligence

BI gives organizations the ability to ask questions in plain language and get answers they can understand. Instead of using best guesses, they can base decisions on what their business data is telling them, whether it relates to production, supply chain, customers, or market trends. Why are sales dropping in this region? Where do we have excess inventory? What are customers saying on social media? BI helps answer such critical questions as these.

BI provides past and current insights into a business. This is achieved via an array of technologies and practices that range from descriptive analytics and reporting to data mining, forecasting, and predictive analytics. By providing an accurate picture of the business at a specific point in time, BI enables an organization to design a business strategy based on factual data.

BI helps organizations become data-driven enterprises, improve performance, and gain competitive advantage. Organizations can:

- Improve ROI by understanding the business and intelligently allocating resources to meet strategic objectives.

- Unravel customer behavior, preferences, and trends, and use the insights to better target prospects or tailor products to changing market needs.

- Monitor business operations, resolve problems, or make improvements on an ongoing basis, fueled by data insights.

- Improve supply-chain management by monitoring activity up and down the line and communicating results with partners and suppliers.

Retailers, for example, can increase cost savings by comparing performance and benchmarks across stores, channels, and regions. Likewise, with visibility into the claims process, insurers can see where they are missing service targets and use that information to improve outcomes.

Business Intelligence Best Practices

Organizations benefit when they can fully assess operations and processes, understand their customers, gauge the market, and drive improvement. They need the right tools to aggregate business information from anywhere, analyze it, discover patterns, and find solutions.

The best BI software supports this decision-making process by:

- Connecting to a wide variety of different data systems and data sets, including databases and spreadsheets

- Providing deep analysis, thereby helping users uncover hidden relationships and patterns in their data

- Presenting answers in informative and compelling data visualizations like reports, maps, charts, and graphs

- Enabling side-by-side comparisons of data under different scenarios

- Providing drill-down, drill-up, and drill-through features, enabling users to investigate different levels of data

Advanced BI and analytics systems may also integrate AI and ML to automate and streamline complex tasks. These capabilities further accelerate the ability of enterprises to analyze their data and gain insights at a deep level.

Consider, for example, how IBM Cognos Analytics brings together data analysis and visual tools to support map creation for reports. The system uses AI to automatically identify geographical information. It can then refine visualizations by adding geospatial mapping of the entire globe, an individual neighborhood, or anything in between.

The Impact of the Lakehouse on BI

Combining the best features, capabilities, cost/performance characteristics, and other attributes of an enterprise data warehouse and a data lake, a lakehouse offering such as watsonx.data makes BI more effective. A lakehouse enables a

BI solution to access more of an enterprise's trusted and valued data so that AI systems can discover and reveal deeper business insights and opportunities.

As mentioned in an earlier chapter, how a lakehouse is built determines its effectiveness. An effective lakehouse architecture is shown in Figure 7.1 and should offer the key capabilities of:

- Scaling for BI across all data with multiple high-performance query engines optimized for different workloads (for example: Presto, Spark, Db2, Netezza, etc.)

- Enabling data sharing between these different engines

- Offering shared common data storage across data lake and data warehouse functions, avoiding unnecessary time-consuming ETL/ELT jobs

- Eradicating unnecessary data duplication and replication

- Leveraging an open and flexible architecture built on open source without vendor lock-in

- Deploying across hybrid cloud environments (on-premises, private, public clouds) on multiple hyperscalers

- Offering a wide range of prebuilt integration capabilities incorporating data-fabric capabilities.

- Offering organizations the flexibility to start their lakehouse implementations standalone and later expand to a bigger integrated AI and data platform

- Providing global governance and security across all data in the hybrid multi-cloud enterprise leveraging data-fabric capabilities

- Being extensible through APIs, strong value-add partner ecosystems, accelerators, and third-party solutions

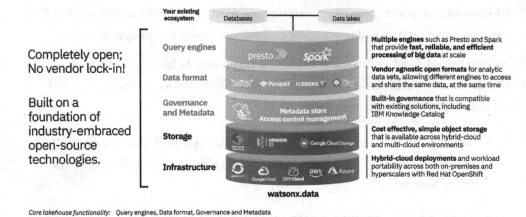

Figure 7.1: An effective lakehouse architecture for BI

8

CONCLUSION

Data is at the center of every business. It keeps applications running, powers predictive insights, and enables better experiences for customers and employees. However, the full benefit of data is elusive because of the way data is stored and accessed for analytics and AI.

Enterprises that rely on monolithic repositories with multiple data warehouses and data lakes located on premises and on cloud are far from alone. Based on many IBM engagements, more than 80 percent of organizations are inhibited by data silos. History has shown that the amount of stored data will continue to grow at an accelerated rate.

The data lake was supposed to fix all these issues; just land company data in a centralized place and process it. But it's not so easy to update the lakes, properly catalog data, or ensure good governance—and the skillsets required for these tasks are specific, rare, and expensive. As a result, data lakes have proven more costly to build and maintain than originally perceived. A data warehouse does offer high performance for processing terabytes of structured data, but warehouses can become expensive, too, especially for new and evolving workloads. Most organizations run analytics and AI workloads in ecosystems that are complex and cost-inefficient. It's time for a change.

For AI to be adopted by the masses, it needs to be accessible and as easy to use as turning on a light switch. Users must be able to rely on it. Trust it. Let it do its thing. To do that, though, AI needs to be able to access and consume its life source (all data) simply so that it can apply its models intelligently and transparently, enabling businesses to discover and act on insights to produce smarter business outcomes.

A lakehouse combines the best capabilities and features of data lakes and data warehouses. A lakehouse has the potential to be a one-stop shop for an enterprise to store and access all of its data. In our opinion, a lakehouse that is built on an architecture that uses open standards, open-source components, and execution engines that are optimized for different workloads will enable AI systems to access everything they need. This could potentially make those AI systems become close to being sentient within the enterprise. For these reasons, the lakehouse might be one of the most important data management advances since the birth of the Relational Database Management System (RDBMS) in 1983.

Of course, governance—whether general governance, data governance, or AI—will remain central to the success of implementing a lakehouse. AI, data, and governance are symbiotic, like the three legs of a tripod. If one leg fails, the other two fall over and the whole thing comes tumbling down.

AI cannot exist without information architecture (IA). An IA such as a data fabric forms a crucial foundation for a client's data infrastructure, facilitating the realization of AI's benefits. Its primary function is to gather, prepare, and organize data, making it readily available for consumption. This data preparation is crucial for maximizing an organization's AI capabilities. Once the data is properly organized, it can be readily accessed and used by AI builders using watsonx—more specifically, watsonx.ai and watsonx.data.

Cloud Pak for Data serves as a comprehensive integrated technology platform that forms the foundation for many data and AI capabilities. Built on Red Hat OpenShift, the platform offers a standardized set of essential services. Key functions like security, authentication, and logging are already integrated. These foundational Cloud Pak for Data services form the backbone of watsonx services, facilitating the consumption of these data assets for AI purposes, as shown in Figure 8.1.

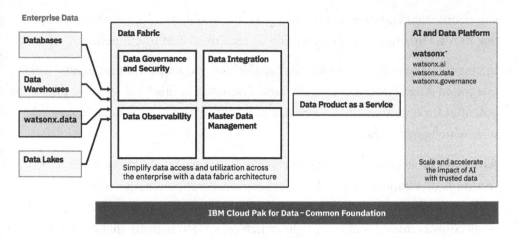

Figure 8.1: Cloud Pak for Data as a shared foundation for data and AI services

The data product lifecycle is simplified as follows:

1. On the left side of the diagram, the client's enterprise data is stored in numerous data repositories, from which a client could implement watsonx.data to serve its data lakehouse needs.

2. A data fabric can be implemented to discover the data and create an enriched view of the metadata associated with those sources, determine quality and lineage, and understand governance policies that should be applied to that data.

3. Curated data products can be crafted from the data fabric and published for access by data consumers via the data product hub.

4. AI builders can use the watsonx platform to consume the data products for their AI projects, including bringing their data products into watsonx.data for simplified consumption.

This integrated tool chain is possible due to the common foundation provided by Cloud Pak for Data. This approach is designed to help organizations be more successful with AI.

Organizational culture plays an important role in adopting and implementing AI. We could write an entire chapter (or even a book) on this subject, but we choose to leave that discussion for a different day. Simply put, organizations and people that embrace and trust AI have the potential to outperform those that don't. Organizations that don't do so face the threat of extinction.

In closing, lakehouses that offer the capabilities and that form part of an integrated AI and data system like those discussed in this book provide the potential for organizations of any size to leverage AI as a consumable service with which anyone can interact.

AI should be as easy as driving a vehicle without having to know the inner workings of a combustion or electrical engine. AI should be perceived as reliable, trustworthy, and as safe as traveling in an airliner. AI should also be as consumable as flicking a light switch on a wall, trusting that the light will enable everyone to see more clearly. Simply ask an AI system a question or give it a task and it will do the work faster, more accurately, and more intelligently than humans alone.

In summary, we believe AI is the key to business enlightenment. It can help us step out of the dark, unwrapping the DNA buried deep within our organization's data and business processes to produce the most revealing and deepest insights that help us achieve smarter business outcomes.

For those yet to venture into AI, we started this book with a quote from Confucius, so we think it only apt to also finish with one:

> *"The journey of 1,000 miles begins with a single step."*

NOTICES AND DISCLAIMERS

Azure is a registered trademark of Microsoft Corporation. www.microsoft.com/en-us/legal/intellectualproperty/trademarks/en-us.aspx

Google is a registered trademark of Google LLC. www.google.com/permissions/trademark/trademark-list/

Kubernetes is a registered trademark of The Linux Foundation. https://www.linuxfoundation.org/trademark-list/

Python is a registered trademark of the Python Software Foundation. www.python.org/psf/trademarks/

Red Hat, OpenShift are registered trademark of Red Hat Inc. www.redhat.com/en/about/trademark-guidelines-and-policies

RStudio is a trademark of RStudio, Inc. https://www.rstudio.com/about/trademark/

Jupyter is a trademark of the NumFOCUS foundation, of which Project Jupyter is a part. https://jupyter.org/governance/trademarks.html